Lessons from Mom

Lessons from

A Tribute to Loving Wisdom

Joan Aho Ryan

Health Communications, Inc.
Deerfield Beach, Florida

We would like to acknowledge the following publishers and individuals for permission to reprint the material below. (Note: The stories that were penned anonymously, that are in the public domain or were written by Joan Aho Ryan are not included in this listing. We exercised due diligence, but failed to locate the copyright holder of *The Parrot*. Please contact us if you are the copyright holder of this item.)

Rhubarb Pie. Reprinted by permission of Health Communications, Inc. from *Values from the Heartland* by Bettie B. Youngs. ©1995 Bettie B. Youngs.

My Mother, Mrs. Smith. From *The Mother Book* by Liz Smith. ©1978 by Liz Smith. Published by Doubleday & Company, Inc.

The Invisible Wound. Reprinted by permission of Loreen Stipp Wade. ©1985 by Loreen Stipp Wade.

When Words Fail, Children Hope Gifts Say Enough. Reprinted with permission of *The Miami Herald*. ©1996 Leonard Pitts Jr.

An Angel on Earth. Reprinted by permission of Nora Tripp. ©1996 Nora Tripp.

A Woman I Admire. Reprinted by permission of Barnard College and Ivellisse Rodriguez. ©1995. Ms. Rodriguez is a winner of the 1995 Barnard College Essay Contest.

My Worst Mother's Day Ever. Reprinted by permission of Deborah Smoot. ©1996 Deborah Smoot.

Library of Congress Cataloging-in-Publication Data

Cataloging-in-Publication data is
available from the Library of Congress.

©1996 Joan Aho Ryan
ISBN 1-55874-386-3

Publisher: Health Communications, Inc.
          3201 S.W. 15th Street
          Deerfield Beach, Florida 33442-8190

Cover design by Jose Villavicencio

*She broke the bread into two fragments
and gave them to the children, who ate with avidity.
"She hath kept none for herself," grumbled the Sergeant.
"Because she is not hungry," said a soldier.
"Because she is a mother," said the Sergeant.*

Victor Hugo

With love, I dedicate this book to my mother, Ann Aho, who is the embodiment of the mother described by Victor Hugo. The mother of 12 children, with ten surviving, she spent a lifetime sacrificing for her children, without complaint.

Now 85 years old and blind for several years, she continues to dispense the love and wisdom that is at the heart of this book. While the world is a vastly different place from the one she knew as a younger mother, that other private world between mother and child is unchanged. It is a quiet place of caring, nurturing and unconditional love.

Thank you, Mom, for making that place for me for so many years. And for teaching me that this is the beginning of all love.

—Joan Aho Ryan

*I really learned it all
from mothers.*

—Dr. Benjamin Spock

Contents

Acknowledgments

My mother inspired this book, but her contribution was only the first in a long process. Without the support, encouragement and contributions of so many others, the "lessons" would have remained just an idea for a book I might one day produce. I want to especially thank other members of my family for making it a reality.

Heartfelt thanks to: My sister, Diane, and her husband, Jim, for their unfailing willingness to be of help—no matter what the circumstances. I have never known two people more generous or caring. I am thankful to them for so many things, including taking care of Mom for all of us. Being part of your lives, and getting to know Chris, has enriched us.

My daughter, Diana, whose compassion and tenderness for all creatures are a real lesson in mothering. I am blessed with a daughter who is not only precious to me but works to make the world a better place.

My sister, Pat, for being excited about this book from the beginning and cheering me on. I am grateful to her for propping me up—as she has so many times.

My brother, Tom, and his wife, Eva, who made some sacrifices so we could pursue a dream. I know you will protest, but we owe you.

My stepdaughter, Erica Ress, whose talent as a writer is matched by her generosity of spirit. Thanks, Erica, for enlisting your friends on my behalf.

There are many others who believed in this project, and gave me their support in numerous ways. Some went the extra mile for me: Yustin Wallrapp, who not only delivered when I asked for his help, but got it right and, as he often does, raised the bar.

Jill and Joel Kimmel, who didn't hesitate to help, and opened their hearts.

Ron Levy of North American Precis, who knows how to be a friend and runs the best editorial service in the world. You have my endorsement on both counts, Ron, any time.

Liz Smith, who made my day when she graciously gave me permission to use her wonderful story about her mother, Mrs. Smith.

Intrepid pilot George Burns, who's also a thoroughly kind man and, as I recall, a helluva speechwriter.

Allan Kalmus, who probably learned how to be a good and loyal friend from his extraordinary mother.

Debbie Smoot, who surely doesn't need her byline published yet one more time—but who responded enthusiastically and has very special credentials as a writer and a mom. Thank you, Debbie.

My thanks to all the others around the country who made *Lessons from Mom* possible. Contributors often accompanied the stories and poems that are part of this collection with heartfelt good wishes for the success of the project, and I appreciated all the kind words.

Special thanks to Gary Seidler of Health Communications, who gave me the opportunity to present the concept for this book, and Peter Vegso for endorsing it and moving it forward. Christine Belleris and Matthew Diener have been sensitive and insightful editors, and I thank them for keeping me focused and skillfully pulling it all together. Finally, my thanks to Kim Weiss and Randee Goldsmith, the talented PR team at Health Communications, for their enthusiasm and commitment to publicizing the book.

Above all, I want to acknowledge the love and support of my husband and friend, Jack. His natural optimism and innate goodness have helped me believe in myself and all good things despite tough times. I was lucky enough to marry the man of my dreams and, after 25 years, he is still my hero.

Introduction

Lessons from Mom began as a very personal exchange between my mother and me. I wanted to acknowledge, after many years, a debt of gratitude to her for raising me to believe that the beginning of all virtue is weighing the moral significance of one's actions. By her own example she taught me that making judgments about right and wrong is often difficult, but it's the only path to building character, behaving decently towards others and assuming responsibility for oneself.

During this book's year-and-a-half evolution, it has countless times rewarded me on a personal level with vivid recollections of all the precious "lessons" from my own mother that have strengthened and graced my life.

What was totally unexpected, and gratifying on another level, was the tremendous appeal this book evidently held for so many people. Numerous individuals wrote me to say *Lessons from Mom* was a great idea because there is more to our lives than the violence and unhappiness we see in today's headlines or watch showcased on talk shows. From people all over the country, and of all ages and backgrounds, I was encouraged to get the word out that love, kindness, courage, compassion, patience and so many other virtues are alive and well—despite what we read in the newspapers, watch on television or see at the movie theaters.

And that gratification increased every month, as stories and poems celebrating motherly love and wisdom began arriving from every part of the country—from rural Tennessee to major urban centers like New York and Los Angeles, and from all over the vast heartland of America. Over and over again, contributors sounded the same theme of a mother teaching values and virtues the old-fashioned way, by example and with consistency, firmness and love.

There are lessons in this book for all of us, men and women, young and old. Whether funny or sad, I hope they will warm your heart and, as they have for me, remind you of some precious moments with your own mother.

Pundits and social critics of every era have sounded alarms about the demise of civilization, and the lack of morality and virtue in the land. We're certainly hearing a lot about this in America today. I don't know whether things are any worse than they were at some other period in our history, but I do know these stories seem to offer the kind of positive, life-affirming messages that resonate with people of all ages and backgrounds. The theme of a mother's love and wisdom is universal and timeless.

Transcending the personal and perhaps enriching other people's lives with these stories is, for me, the most gratifying part of producing this book. I hope you enjoy it.

Mother o' Mine

(Dedication to *The Light that Failed*)

If I were hanged on the highest hill,
Mother o' mine, O mother o' mine!
I know whose love would follow me still,
Mother o' mine, O mother o' mine!

If I were drowned in the deepest sea,
Mother o' mine, O mother o' mine!
I know whose tears would come down to me,
Mother o' mine, O mother o' mine!

If I were damned of body and soul,
I know whose prayer would make me whole,
Mother o' mine, O mother o' mine!

Rudyard Kipling

A Good Day's Work

*I go on working for the same reason
that a hen goes on laying eggs.*

—H. L. Mencken

Observing my mother over the past three years illuminated for me precisely why I've never been able to stop working at something or other. For years, I assumed there was either a missing part or one part too many that made it impossible for me to stay home. Despite the fact that I was a single mother, obliged to earn a living and support my daughter and myself, I had overwhelming feelings of guilt about the fact that I actually found it interesting and fulfilling to go to work.

Those feelings were certainly fueled by the fact that there weren't too many mothers of young children out in the workplace in the 1960s and 1970s. I remember, vividly in fact, that Diana was the only little girl in nursery school whose parents were divorced, and whose Mommy didn't pick her up in the afternoon.

After all these years of wondering what was wrong with me, Mom helped me understand why working was so important to me, beyond the obvious need to collect a paycheck. She taught me by her example.

One day I suggested she might help one of my clients by stuffing envelopes for a monthly mailing to their customers. Since she lost her vision very late in life—well into her 70s—my mother was never willing to learn Braille or any of the coping skills blind people are taught. As a result, while she's fiercely independent and self-reliant, she is apprehensive about taking on any challenges beyond her simple and unvaried daily routine.

Quite predictably, she was very doubtful of her ability to handle this assignment. I, on the other hand, had complete confidence that she had the manual dexterity, motivation and energy, and that it would be a positive experience for her.

What's happened, of course, is that Mom now waits for her twice-a-week delivery of envelopes and mailing pieces. Since she's paid a set amount for every 100 envelopes she stuffs, she's begun to work faster so she can exceed her previous month's wages every month.

When I see her put herself into position to begin her work, I see a person transformed. The lethargy that sets in from "watching" television (she listens to talk shows during the day) absolutely disappears. To the extent that a blind 85-year-old woman can leap across the room, she leaps to the chair at her small round table, and her hands almost caress the stacks of envelopes and mailers in front of her. When the stacks are high, she exults. Sometimes, she'll ask me if the upcoming project is "for big envelopes or small." When I say "big," she is very pleased because she can work faster with the big ones.

Apart from having something to do on a regular basis, she is enthralled with the idea that she is earning money. Even now, months since she began stuffing envelopes, she boasts to anyone she's in contact with about how much she is earning each month. Everyone in her condominium complex knows she has a job. Last month she asked me if she could have some time off while my sister was visiting with her. Asking for time off is not only part of her work ethic, it's also confirmation that she has real responsibilities and is being held accountable. She wants to know, like all of us, that what she does has some meaning.

When she began this work, my mother was fearful. Now she's disappointed if it's not a very large mailing, and she asks me almost daily when the next mailing will be. In the beginning, she was concerned if she had to use paper clips to hold the mailing pieces together before inserting them in the envelopes. She was certain that would be an extra step she couldn't handle. Now she looks forward to every variation that will challenge her. Envelopes with clasps that need to be closed, for example, are preferable to gummed flaps. Odd-shaped inserts that need special folding are among her favorites. "Who needs eyes," she jauntily asks, while stuffing away.

Above all, what I've learned from Mom about work is how absolutely human and ordinary it was for me to almost lose my mind when I was unemployed or otherwise not working. Now I know that some of the dumbest, most irrational things I've done were associated with feeling lost, without purpose, bored and worthless—all the casebook feelings ascribed to not having any work to do.

Mom has made me understand that I don't have an extra career gene or a missing mother gene. Instead, all I have is a deep and universal need to feel useful. It's exactly the same need I had at 30, certainly have in middle-age and, as my mother and so many of her generation have proved, will probably have at 80. At least I hope so.

If I ever doubted how important that is, my mother's constant inquiry—"Have you any work for me today?"—would persuade me. She needs that work as much as she needs the meals we bring her.

No one has taught me more about the value of work. And no one would be more surprised than my mother to know she's still teaching me.

Joan Aho Ryan

Rhubarb Pie

No mean woman can cook well, for it calls for a light head, a generous spirit, and a large heart.

—Paul Gauguin

Our farm, with a sprawling 40 acres of homestead, was ideal for our large family of six children and the many pets who considered themselves one of us.

A half-acre garden grew to the east of our house; to the right of the garden grew the rhubarb patch. The garden received mixed reviews. It produced fresh vegetables, but it also needed constant attention and occasionally we children had to "serve time" in the garden—for an injustice committed or just to keep idle hands busy—hoeing and pulling weeds. With the rhubarb patch, however, all associations were positive.

The rhubarb patch never required weeding. So determined to dominate this little plot of soil, each and every spring—according to Mother Nature's time clock—the rhubarb sprouted forth, pushing aside and crowding out any weed that dared get in its way. Aesthetically, with enormous rich green leaves and tall, hearty stalks painted in various hues of pink, green and purple, the rhubarb plants were quite a regal sight.

Aside from being willful and majestic, the plants were also mysterious and enchanting. From dusk to dawn, the heavily veined leaves of the mature plants drooped themselves over the tightly coiled baby leaves as though to protect them and to allow the tiny leaves to suckle droplets of their dripping dew. But as planet Earth made its daily rotation to face the Sun, the larger leaves abandoned their caretaking roles and instead turned their long necks skyward to bask in the glorious morning light. Now exposed, the smaller leaves were seduced into awakening; slowly they unfolded their palms and drank in the rays, nourishing their fruit below.

Beauty deceived their taste! Saying that a young, tender stalk of raw rhubarb tastes significantly better than does a mature stalk, while true, isn't saying much. And we children knew first hand. "Last one to the house (or the barn, mailbox, shed, school, bus, garden, you name it) has to eat an entire stalk of rhubarb! Amongst my brothers and sisters, being a "rotten egg" for finishing last in a dare wasn't enough; having to eat a stalk of the tart, acidic rhubarb was far and away more of an incentive to join in the game and to cooperate competitively!

We children knew well the taste of rhubarb—both raw, and cooked and sweetened as a dessert.

In the spring and summer my mother performed the seasonal ritual of harvesting the young tender stalks. I often watched her gather them: long coffee-brown hair loosely tied back with a ribbon, joyously humming and singing as she went about selecting the best of the stalks from the patch, carefully laying them in the flowered apron that protected her full-skirted, flower-print dress.

The lovely vision of my mother gathering the rhubarb took second place only to the life she helped them lead once they reached our kitchen. Here Mother transformed the tart stalk into scrumptious pies and puddings and other desserts for our family. Those that weren't immediately used were placed into plastic bags and began their hibernation in the freezer, awaiting their turn for use in the late fall and winter months.

Our family loved the way Mother prepared desserts from rhubarb and looked forward to the time when they were served. Of these, our favorite was the rhubarb pie. This is not to say it was the only pie we enjoyed; goodness knows there were many—cherry, blueberry, mulberry, blackberry, strawberry, peach, apple and pecan—all made by my mother, yet none had the following of her rhubarb pie. Perhaps this was because the rhubarb pie, as Mother made it, was absolutely delicious—and because we knew and appreciated the time and toil involved, the rhubarb pie was symbolic of our mother's loving willingness to do for her family.

Often the rhubarb desserts were prepared by Mother's efforts alone; at other times she involved us fully in the process. Sometimes we made rhubarb-strawberry pudding or rhubarb-custard pudding or other variations, but making the pastry for the rhubarb pie, and filling it, was our most favorite thing to do. Always teaching, Mother showed us how to wash the long stalks and carefully cut them into 1/2-inch cubes, enough for the 3 cups needed for a rhubarb pie (sometimes two or three pies were made at the same time). These were placed in a bowl and mixed with 1 cup of sugar, 1 teaspoon of ground cinnamon (or 2 table-spoons of chopped candied ginger), 1 tablespoon of butter, 1 egg and 1 tablespoon of cornstarch. This mixture was then set aside and we turned our attention to making the pie crust.

Meticulously, our mother taught us how to accurately measure out the cup and a half of flour, 6 tablespoons of butter, 1/4 cup of water and the half teaspoon of salt needed for the pie crust. Patiently, she helped us learn how to roll out the pastry larger than the pie dish, cut away the outer strip of pastry, lay it on the dampened rim of the dish and brush it with water.

At this point the fruit mixture was packed into the pie dish, mounding it high in the middle, and the "pastry lid" was laid over the filling and trimmed to fit the unbaked pie. As a finishing touch, Mother decorated the pie crust by pinching the dough on the rim into small, even scallops, and allowed each child to use a knife to make one small slit in the pastry top to allow steam to escape during cooking.

Mother then placed the pie in the oven and set the timer. While the pie was baking, we children embarked on another exciting venture—left-over dough was rolled, pummeled, slapped, twisted, poked and shaped into designs of our own imaginations. On these we sprinkled candied sugars, raisins, nuts and chocolate chips (sometimes pieces of carrot strips and peas or small pieces of rhubarb were used for eyes or buttons or for decorations). Our "do-dads," as we called them, were then placed on a flat baking tin and put into the oven—though many were eaten raw and never reached the oven!

Brrring! Finally, the timer announced the magical moment we'd all been waiting for and we all gathered around to see what the oven had done to our pie. The fruits of our labor were about to be realized. Breathlessly we watched as Mother removed our masterpiece from the oven and placed it on the table. Seeing it in all its golden majesty and inhaling its warm, sweet aroma gave each one of us a great sense of accomplishment. For small children, the feeling of mastery and satisfaction was nothing less than what Michelangelo experienced when at last he completed his paintings on the ceiling of the Sistine Chapel. Our pie was perfect. We needed only to look at our mother's smiling face for confirmation.

Perhaps because the rhubarb pie was always present for holidays, birthdays and other special events, it became synonymous with joy and festivity. Whatever the reason, the rhubarb pie was ever-popular, and grew in stature and importance as time went by. Soon we all left home and began lives of our own. But we returned to the family nest to share our joys, our woes—and rhubarb pie. Later, when we adult children brought home spouses and children of our own, a rhubarb pie was always prepared as a homecoming and greeted us from the middle of the kitchen table as we entered the family home. And when we were ready to leave, there—accompanying hugs, wet eyes and third-time good-byes, nestled beside a care basket of homemade breads, jams and kringlas[1]—sat a rhubarb pie, no doubt prepared and then hidden away for the occasion of departure.

The rhubarb pie became symbolic of Burres family unity in celebration and comfort. It endures today—a symbol of taste, time, togetherness.

It is hard, though not impossible, to find rhubarb in all grocery

---

1. A Norwegian pastry often served with coffee or tea. It takes the place of cake or cookies.

stores. And it can't be found in all restaurants, but in some it will be on the menu. Maybe you will want to remedy this as I have; I've planted my own rhubarb patch. And every time I go out to pick from it, I wear my mother's flowered apron, the many-times-patched one that I begged her to give me when she said it had seen its finest hour. And I hum and sometimes sing as I prune the patch or pick from it—with the intent of making a pie or giving some of the beautiful stalks to a friend, or sometimes just to call forth the lovely sight of my mother gathering the rhubarb in her apron and, with her children gathered around, rolling pie crust with her mother's mother's rolling pin.

Though I can make a mean rhubarb pie, it just doesn't quite taste like the one that my mother serves. So when I make rhubarb pie, I call her just to tell her how much I enjoyed all those rhubarb pies and the work that went with them. And how wonderful it is to be her daughter.

Bettie B. Youngs

My Mother, Mrs. Smith

*True love is like ghosts, which everybody
talks about but few have seen.*

—La Rochefoucauld

When I look at a recent picture of my 84-year-old mother and then look back at the sepia-tinted photographs of her at 16 in a Mississippi State College gym costume, or on her wedding day in 1914, *I see exactly the same woman.*

Poet Anne Sexton wrote, "A woman *is* her mother." And it is true, for when I look at my mother's pictures, young or old, I see something of myself in all the stages of her face, just as I see her fleetingly sometimes when I pass a mirror. But I only see the similarity physically.

My mother has always been painfully consistent in her character and personality. I have been zigging and zagging all over the place and have had about a thousand total changes of persona. I admire my mother's serenity and her deep convictions, but her certainties are not for me.

Mothers and daughters who are able to be honest about themselves will admit that, however much they may love and be devoted, a high pain quotient is exchanged. My mother was never jealous or envious of me but caused me a great deal of pain because the standards she lived by were so idealistic and moral that I simply could not live up to them. And I caused my mother

12

a lot of pain because I was nobody's idea of a darling daughter. I was rebellious and offbeat.

The word has fallen into disrepute now. Nevertheless, "lady" is the word inextricably bound up with "mother" in this daughter's mind. The issue of being a lady and behaving in a ladylike manner was occasionally appealing, more often distressing, when I was growing up.

And my father's old-fashioned attitudes supplied the reinforcement my mother required for her views on ladylike behavior, civilized demeanor, manners and mores. My father believed there were only two kinds of women—ladies and the other kind. One of the reasons he married my mother, of course, was because he was a poor, uneducated boy from the hardscrabble West Texas plains and she was a soft-spoken, magnolia-voiced lady whose gentility appealed to his rougher background. My parents were, in fact, classic lovers—an incredible case of opposites attracting. He was short, she was stately; he was ugly, she was beautiful; she never lost her temper, he never kept his; she was naive, he was street-smart.

When a tall, gorgeous Southern belle with a full bosom and bright blue eyes marries a short, strung-out, runty-looking little live wire, one may well wonder why. "I was in love with him," she says simply.

My mother remembers that my father was "fun" and "different" from the other nice boys her doctor brothers were introducing her to in Ennis, Texas. They had imported her fresh from college to keep house for them. As next-door neighbors, Sloan Smith and Elizabeth McCall began to date. They married. He went on buying cotton, which was his trade, and spent almost 50 years trying to change my mother into an energetic, impulsive, live-for-the-moment Texan. She remained stubbornly the lovely thing he had most prized her for—a lady, slow, gentle, cultured and worried about what the neighbors would say.

When my parents were in a car wreck which broke my mother's neck, I rushed to the hospital where she was in traction. The sight of her suffering was unbearable, but I went to the bed and, leaning over her, whispered, "Well, how was your underwear?" She searched my face, puzzled, then started laughing. "Oh, honey," she said, "I had on my new Christmas things. It was all right."

My parents almost never agreed on anything. My mother wanted a home with music, books, several bathrooms and annuities tucked away for college educations. My father bought polo ponies, brought home hitchhikers, lent all his money.

My father's penchant for gambling almost drove my mother crazy, since she thought it was sinful, immoral and wasteful. One day I found her with the mail in her hand, crying. I asked what was the matter. "Oh," she said, "I just can't bear the thought of *The Daily Racing Form* and *The Baptist Standard* in the same mailbox."

My father was so sharp and fast that I recall as a child cringing night after night as he beat my mother in whatever game they were playing—dominoes, gin, checkers, canasta. I used to cross my fingers and pray, "This time, let her win." I mistakenly felt sorry for her and hadn't a clue that she had no more desire to win than to wear pants.

When my father died at 74, I was long grown up and had spent a deluded lifetime of seeing my parents as inextricably unsuited, unhappy even. Except for their curious agreement about daughters being ladylike, I always felt they had been drastically mismatched.

But in the days following his funeral, I saw that theirs had been a real romance, a love match of such satisfaction to both of them that it never mattered that their children were too ignorant to see it. The reality of my mother's loss, her love, her grief and her satisfaction at having loved the same man for almost 50 years was overwhelming.

I had never really appreciated my mother until then. I had always definitely been Daddy's girl. In the time I spent at home after my father's death I received a kind of great awakening and a gift—the full realization of my mother's worth, her wonder, her splendor. My father had gone on wherever he had to go, but he had left behind his love for my mother, and to my great happiness, I was able to make it my own. I have had the most incredibly fulfilling relationship with my mother since then. I would wish every daughter such a happy experience.

Liz Smith

The Invisible Wound

I know I am but summer to your heart,
and not the full four seasons of the year.

—Edna St. Vincent Millay

My mother died tragically, and by her own hand, when I was 17 and she was 49. On that lovely spring morning, our eyes had met as I left the dining room table and headed down the hall to the bathroom to insert my contact lenses. There was something so haunting and sad in her expression, as though she wanted to say something but couldn't find the words. Standing in the bathroom behind the closed door, I heard the explosion as it reverberated through the house. I rushed back to the dining room and then into my mother's bedroom. Her lifeless body was sprawled on the floor, a gun beside her.

Mom had often told me I was special—her favorite, because I was the last of six children she had brought into the world. For many years after that terrible spring morning, I searched for answers to questions that tortured me. Why did she leave me? Didn't she love me? How could she? I sank deeper and deeper into guilt, self-pity and resentment. The pain was unbearable.

Now that we understand so much more about the severe mental depression my mother suffered from, I realize how inappropriate those questions were. I know she loved me. She did not choose to leave me. I know now that she was in terrible pain,

15

which the world could not see because it was so far beneath the surface and there was no visible wound. I know now that she had lost hope.

At one time, it would have been impossible for me to offer a tribute to my mother because I could not see beyond my own pain. Today, as I raise two girls of my own—my mother's grand-daughters—I cherish the memories of the love she gave me. I think of how brave she was, and how much she endured. That is the legacy by which I choose to remember my mother.

—*Loreen Stipp Wade*

Little Treasures

The story is told of the young mother putting moisturizer on her face when her little girl asked her what she was doing. Wanting to satisfy her daughter's curiosity about beauty secrets, she carefully explained that the cream was good for wrinkles. Studying her mother's face intently, the little girl replied, "It's doing a great job, Mommy. You've got *so many* wrinkles."

∾

A five-year-old boy had one of those trouble-filled days. After his mother reprimanded him several times for being disobedient, she finally lost patience with his willful behavior.

"Jackie, you go sit down on that chair in the corner right now, and don't get up until I tell you," she said sternly.

The little boy went to the chair, sat down and, after a few minutes, called to his mother.

"Mommy, I'm sitting down on the outside, but I'm standing up on the inside. Is that okay?"

∾

A friend recently told me how her eight-year-old daughter offered solace and comfort to the mother of a playmate who was gravely ill. When she got home, my friend asked her little girl what she had done to make her friend's mother feel better. With the utmost seriousness, the little girl softly replied, "I just sat on her lap and cried with her."

∾

A clever four-year-old developed a deep affection for *The Cat in the Hat* and urged his mother to read it to him every night before bedtime. The mother, worn out from a day at the office and raising three children by herself, bought her son an audio-tape of the story so she wouldn't have to spend time reading it each night. This worked a few times, since he was fascinated by the voice coming out of the player and pushing the buttons himself. Then one evening he called to his mother and, handing her the book, urged her to read *The Cat in the Hat*.

"Now, Billy, I'm surprised at you. You know how to turn on the player."

"Yes," Billy answered, "but I can't sit on its lap."

Anonymous

When Words Fail, Children Hope Gifts Say Enough

*In general, those parents have the
most reverence who deserve it.*

—Samuel Johnson

One of my sons has declared it his goal to someday buy his mother a black BMW trimmed in gold, though we have two perfectly adequate vehicles in the driveway. Another wants to buy her a big house in a nice neighborhood. Never mind that she already has one.

It comes with being a mother's son, I suppose—the burning need to lay treasures at her feet as a way to express the inexpressible: Mother, I am so grateful.

I know that feeling. It rushed in on me a few days ago when business took me to Natchez, Mississippi, where my own mother was born and raised. Driving the narrow streets of the black neighborhoods, I recalled how I dreamed of the riches I'd give her, the triumphs I would wrench from life for no other reason than to see the pride in her smile.

She died before it happened. Seven years later, I still feel this sharp tug of jealousy whenever some young athlete, suddenly a millionaire, declares that his first expense will be a mansion for his mother.

The costliest gift I ever gave mine was a plane ticket. Actually, my sisters and brother and I all chipped in on that, presenting our mother with a round-trip ticket to Natchez.

The ticket was a gift for what was to be her final birthday before cancer won its years-long battle. It seemed woefully inadequate in light of what she had given us: spirit riches in the shadow of poverty; security on the edge of apprehension; a home in a city jungle.

Sick from heart disease and hypertension, abused by a husband who'd sold his soul to the bottle, she gave us *ourselves*. She made us women and men.

What's a plane ticket compared with that?

I had all but forgotten our gesture until a few days ago in Natchez. There, I stopped at the home of Isabel Gordon, my mother's lifelong friend, and we spoke about that last journey home.

Mrs. Gordon said Mom told her, "My life has been really rough. But if I didn't have my children, I don't know what I'd have done. My children sent me home for my birthday. I'd been wanting to come home one more time."

Mrs. Gordon asked if Mom had hinted around for the ticket. "She said, 'No, they did it on their own. And I appreciate it. If I don't get back no more, I've been home for the last time."

It surprised me. I mean, we knew she appreciated the gift, we knew she enjoyed the trip, but we never knew it meant what it did.

She died not long after.

I have no words for the sweetness that suffused the pain as I left that woman's company. None for how high I flew or on what weightless wings.

I had always wondered if she knew. How grateful we were, I mean. We said "I love you," sure. So what? People say that all the time. We gave her perfumes, vases, necklaces and all the other gifts one gives.

But I didn't know if she *knew*.

How do you express the inexpressible? What perfume says, "I appreciate your patience that time you helped me with my math"?

What vase declares, "I'm grateful for the times I slipped out of bed, and we shared a soda and talked awhile before you sent me back"? What necklace expresses, "Thank you for not letting my father hit me"?

I know the answer now. I guess I always did. And I find myself a little less jealous of celebrity athletes, a little more at peace.

I drove around my mother's town that afternoon and felt myself lifted by a realization that came into the day like an unexpected breeze and left a gift of serenity in its wake:

She knew.

Leonard Pitts Jr.

An Angel on Earth

*We could never learn to be brave and patient
if there were only joy in the world.*

—Helen Keller

I have always thought our mother of four was an angel here
on earth. She always had a smile and an ear to listen to anything
we had to tell her. As a young girl, I remember so many times
that she might have become very angry with me, but instead she
would gently try to make me see what I had done wrong.

After I was married and started a family of my own, I realized
how valuable Mother's lessons had been. One day, I was baking
a cake from scratch and our two-year-old was helping me. She
had on a little yellow apron and was standing on a chair close to
where I was mixing the cake's ingredients. As I turned around to
get the baking pan, she began stirring, and stirred the cake mix
right off the table.

As she started to cry, staring at the mixing bowl upside down
on the floor, I tried to envision what Mother would have done.
So I hugged Kathy and told her it was alright, and that we'd just
start all over again. We did, and the cake was probably the best
one ever. I told Kathy she was a good cook and that she would
be my cooking partner from then on.

Patience is what my mother taught me, and I still feel her guiding me into the right decisions every day. My four children are

grown and married now. When we are all together, I see myself and their grandmother in them, and it makes me very happy.

Of the many angels among us every day, it is my mother's wings that I feel the most often, and with the most joy.

Nora Tripp

A Woman I Admire

*Courage is the ladder on which all
the other virtues mount.*

—Clare Booth Luce

It was 1982 and a thin, young woman was moving nervously along the Bronx streets, holding her daughter's hand tightly. She was searching for the nearest hotel, trying not to think about what her husband was going to do when he discovered that she hadn't returned home with their daughter.

She was 22 years old, with medium-length brown hair. There was an ugly bruise on her cheek. At 5'7" she had often been teased about her height, and just now she felt as conspicuous as a totem pole; she wished she were invisible. Her name was Nereida Rosado and she had just left her husband.

As Nereida walked, she carried on a conversation with herself in Spanish about how she was going to survive on the little money she had. "Great! Little one, we have found a hotel. I hope they don't charge too much." She entered under a garish neon sign and walked to the front desk. "How much does it cost to stay here for a night?" my mother asked. The man said, "Fifteen dollars." "Good, then I'll stay here for"—she counted again—"two nights," she said.

Nereida knew that she couldn't stay longer because she would run out of money; worse, she felt instinctively that

24

somehow her husband was going to find her if she stayed in one place. Her next check was due in one week so she had to weigh money and safety. We went to our small, over-heated hotel room and Mommy plopped herself on the well-used bed. Tired of walking and worrying, my mother lay down and went to sleep, and I was glad to nestle close to her. I don't think we even took off our shoes.

For a year her husband continued following her every move, and she was sick at heart. "If he tries to scare me out of my new apartment I think I'll kill him. I'm tired of playing this cat-and-mouse chase. I'm starting to grow a great hatred against this man," my mother said in her poetic way. Moments when we forgot my father and breathed easy were rare treats.

On one such evening we were watching television when suddenly, he was banging on the door very hard and shouting. We panicked and ran to the fire escape. We climbed up the ladder to the second floor and started rapping on the family friend's window. Our neighbor, Mrs. Gonzalez, opened the window and let us in. My mother was so nervous she could not speak. She managed to tell her friend to call the cops and tell them that her husband tried to break in. By the time the police came my father had left. The next week my mother hired a lawyer and won a restraining order. "I hope this restraining order will protect us from your father. He's getting more vicious all the time. There's no way to know when he'll try to hurt us again." I later found out that our neighbors and my aunt all contributed to paying the lawyer's fee.

Soon after my eighth birthday—it was 1986—Nereida placed her hands on my shoulders and said, "This is our fourth year on welfare. If we don't do something we'll spend the rest of our lives this way. I need you to be a big girl for your aunt during the evenings so I can go to school." We had grown so close, and it was just like my mom to be considerate and think to prepare her daughter for any changes that might be upsetting.

In 1987 a moment of great excitement arrived one Saturday morning. Nereida checked the mail and quickly opened the envelope. She scored 50 points above the passing score of the G.E.D. She ran up the stairs and into our apartment, jumping up and down. Her friend Monica was an accountant at Henri Bendel, and as soon as Mommy's diploma arrived, she started there as a bookkeeper.

Over the years, Nereida Rosado took to wearing business suits to work, and matching shoes with high heels. When I first noticed, I said, "Mommy, you look so tall—and so good." She turned from checking herself in the mirror to look me straight in the eyes and she said, "What makes me tall is being your mommy, Ivellisse."

Ivellisse Rodriguez

My Worst Mother's Day Ever

*Give a little love to a child, and you
will get a great deal back.*

—John Ruskin

It was Mother's Day, so our little church was packed. At the door, an usher handed a long-stemmed pink carnation to every female who qualified. ("Are you a mother?" he would ask.)

My arms were already full with my four-year-old's coat and a diaper bag for my one-year-old. Shifting those things onto my right arm, I held the carnation above my head so it wouldn't get smashed, then made my way to a pew where my husband and parents were sitting.

There would be no surprises in the program, I thought. It was the same every year—a sea of pink carnations, eulogies to motherhood and, of course, songs about mommies sung by children who wiggled throughout the program.

But this year a well-meaning Sunday-school teacher had come up with a better idea. She had asked each child to draw a picture of his or her mother, and she made these into slides. After each song, a slide of someone's mother was shown, and the child who had drawn the picture was handed the microphone.

"This is my mommy driving the car. She takes us places." A picture of a happy mom with a smiling red-crayon mouth, looking out of a car window, flashed on the screen behind the pulpit.

"This is my mom cooking dinner." Mom with yellow hair and a ruffled apron came into focus. It was a nice touch.

The drawings varied in detail, but all were sweet and tender. As my turn approached, I grew more and more eager. I knew my four-year-old's drawing would be something wonderful—his mommy standing, say, in a field of flowers.

I was somewhere in the middle of that fantasy when I heard Owen bellow: "This is my mommy washing clothes when she first gets up in the morning." The audience roared with laughter at the drawing on the screen. Like a real pro, Owen waited for the laughter to die down before he added, "But I didn't get her hair right. It sticks up more than that."

I could have died. Guilt took the seat next to me, and self-doubt sat next to him. Is that really how Owen sees me? Should I jump out of bed an hour before everyone else, dress, comb my hair, apply lip gloss?

Before I became a mother, I was downright sure of myself about mothering. When Dave and I were newlyweds, his brother and sister-in-law brought their small boys for Easter dinner. The boys got bored and crawled under the table, under the piano, in and out of adult legs. Later I commented to my husband that when we had children, they would never crawl under the piano; I would bring things for them to do, so they wouldn't be bored. I foresaw color-coded bags hanging on hooks in our garage— each full of new crayons and age-appropriate activities—bags I could grab at a moment's notice so my children would always be happy, learning, never bored.

Now 13 years into mothering, and having had a few of my own children under the piano, I realize how naive I was. My bag consists of a few graham crackers I grab on the way out the door. With three children—Owen is now 13, Emily 10 and Amy 6—I'm into survival.

Motherhood is, at best, a humbling experience. Just the other day, Amy ran into the kitchen with two friends in tow and said, "Mom, you gotta laugh! I told them you have the silliest laugh. You have to let them hear it, so they'll believe me. Laugh, Mom, laugh!"

I've always admired humility in others. I just had no idea the price they paid for it.

A friend tells of an executive and his wife who would come to dinner parties and give their "ten commandments for parenting." Soon they had their first baby, then number two, and they came to parties with "eight rules for parenting." By the time they were raising three teenagers, they had gone from "ten commandments" to "three suggestions."

That's about where I am on this Mother's Day: three suggestions that *might* work, not just for parenting, but for life in general. After all, what are children but small people?

1. *Listen.* My Aunt Lois always listened to us children, no matter what kind of questions we had. With everyone else, we kids talked mostly to kneecaps or belt buckles. But whenever we approached Aunt Lois, we didn't get just an answer, we got Aunt Lois. She would hunker down nose-to-nose with us. We would look into her eyes, smell her perfume. She would always repeat the question back to us to make sure she understood it. She made us feel important. We had something important to ask, something worth bending down and listening to. Aunt Lois gave us self-worth.

2. *Treat people as assets.* I learned this truth from my husband's office manager. A parent of four, Carol is a terrific mom. Her family has great mutual respect and love. One day I asked how she achieved it. Carol said that when she and her husband divorced, she realized she would be raising her children alone. Suddenly she needed them as much as they needed her. They learned to rely on one another. "My children are my best friends, my strongest assets," she said.

The best thing we can do for people—child, friend, co-worker or spouse—is to treat them not as liabilities but as assets. I used to rush to the phone before my children could answer it, fearful they'd say the "wrong" thing. Now I don't care if it's the White House calling. My best work is in those three faces. They are capable, bright people. Assets. I'm proud of them.

3. *Remember, we are all God's children.* Fran, a former neighbor of mine, is the mother of six. Her children all had natural self-confidence. They were achievers but weren't obnoxious about it. When I asked about her children one day, she spoke quietly.

"Oh, Debbi, these are not really my children. They are God's. They're just on loan to me. It's a privilege to know them. I see each of them as an important house guest, some influential person in embryo."

What a wonderful way to look at children. What a wonderful way to look at everyone! For, you see, Mother's Day isn't just for mothers. It's for all of us.

I now have Owen's Mother's Day drawing framed and hanging in my laundry room. It is one of my favorite pictures because I realize it was drawn innocently by a little boy who loves his mother—even when her hair is sticking up.

Deborah Smoot

Glimpses of
Famous People's Moms

Gypsy Rose Lee said that her mother was ruthless. She was a "jungle mother," according to Gypsy, and she knew too well that in a jungle it doesn't pay to be nice. "God will protect us," she often said to Gypsy and her sister, June. "But to make sure," she would add, "carry a heavy club."

G. K. Chesterton, the English author, was hopelessly absent-minded. When he became engaged to be married, he was eager to share the happy news with his mother, to whom he was devoted. He went home and wrote her a long letter. Mrs. Chesterton was touched by her son's devotion, as she knew how much effort he had put into the letter. She knew because she lived in the same house and was in the room with him while he wrote it.

Helen Hayes said her mother drew a distinction between achievement and success. She advised her that "achievement is the knowledge that you have studied and worked hard and done the best that is in you. Success is being praised by others, and that's nice, too, but not as important or satisfying. Always aim for achievement and forget about success."

Ꮿ᎒

Some years ago a mother was carrying her baby over the hills of South Wales. She never reached her destination alive. A blizzard overtook her, and a search party later found her frozen beneath the snow. The searchers were surprised that she did not have outer garments but soon discovered why. She had wrapped them around her baby.

When they unwrapped the child, they found baby David Lloyd George alive and well. David Lloyd George grew up to become the prime minister of Great Britain during World War I and one of England's great statesmen. The vital contribution that he made to humanity was possible because his mother had given her life to save him.

Ꮿ᎒

John Wanamaker, one of America's greatest merchants, was once asked, "What was your most glorious hour?" Answered Wanamaker: "When I was a child and my mother took my two baby hands and folded them in prayer as she pointed me to God."

Ꮿ᎒

Nurse Luella Hennessey, who attended the birth of 27 of Rose Kennedy's grandchildren, claims that the Kennedy mothers have adopted a practice that, through the years, has become a family tradition. They have long "conversations" with their babies the first time they meet. Luella explains:

"When the babies are brought to them after they are born, the mothers start communicating with them intimately. They talk softly to them, telling them the secrets they've had in their hearts the last nine months, explaining how much they were wanted, how anxious their brothers and sisters are to see them.

"What astonishes me always is the reaction of the babies. They will look up at the faces of their mothers, as though seeing them and hearing their words. Actually, they *do* hear. The soft, soothing tones, I am convinced, seep into some level of the babies' immature consciousness and they respond.

"I don't know whether one Kennedy mother passed this little custom on to another, but they all do it."

∾

Emily Post, before she became famous as an arbiter of etiquette, tried her hand at many kinds of writing. One of the periodicals to which she submitted material was the original *Life,* which was a humor magazine. Since she was a neophyte at joke-writing, Mrs. Post worked out a system. Before sending a new joke to the editors, she would read it aloud to her mother. If the older woman laughed, Mrs. Post threw out the joke. If her mother looked blank—or better still, disapproving—Mrs. Post slipped it into an envelope and mailed it. Through the years, this system proved infallible.

Anonymous

To Be a Woman

The road to the heart is the ear.

—Voltaire

Elsewhere, spring is announced by a robin or a yellow crocus. But in Brighton Beach, a mostly Jewish enclave on the ocean tip of Brooklyn, New York, you know it's spring when the canvas folding chairs begin to bloom once again in the sidewalk patches of sunlight. The old ladies reappear, clustering in their chairs for a bit of warmth from the sun and from each other. They diagnose one another's winter ailments, they complain of sons and daughters who don't visit often enough and they count their blessings—their grandchildren.

My grandmother used to sit out on the sidewalk like that. Perhaps because my mother will never look as old to me as my grandmother once did, I'm always a little startled to find her among the group of graying women when I visit in the spring.

I'm grateful that she has the companionship of these women, and through her I've come to know them. As we walk to her apartment I learn that one woman has arthritis, another cheats at canasta, a third has a new granddaughter.

Sometimes my mother will say to me, "You know Rose, my upstairs neighbor? She read your article last month. She thought it was wonderful." That's my mother's way of telling me that she liked the article herself. It's part of the code in which we talk to each other.

With the things that count and in the sentences that are supposed to tell how we feel about each other, my mother and I
always speak indirectly. I will say, "The baby really missed you
when we didn't see you last month." She will say, "Aunt Regina
thinks you're looking tired."

Why are we so awkward about saying outright that we miss
each other and worry about each other? Perhaps it's the price an
immigrant mother pays for doing her job too well, working so
hard to give her children an education and new opportunities.
She opens doors for them through which she cannot go herself,
and there is ever afterward a gap not only between generations
but also between cultures.

Or perhaps it's more than a matter of simple sociology. I sus-
pect that our reticence is a great deal more personal.

When I see my mother kissing and cuddling her grandchildren,
I wonder if she ever did that to me. She must have, no matter
how busy she was, working in my father's store, but I don't
remember it. Instead, what I do remember is being seven years
old and coming down with scarlet fever. My mother put cool,
damp cloths on my burning forehead and promised she would
take care of me. But the next day I was rushed by ambulance to
the quarantine ward of a hospital.

I was scared and lonely under the high ceilings of that big white
ward. The nurses clicked along with starched smiles by day, and
two or three of the other young patients cried themselves to sleep
at night. When my mother came to visit, we had to shout at each
other through a partition of glass. I couldn't tell her how I felt
because I was embarrassed to have the other little girls hear.
Instead, I grew more and more furious with my mother for having abandoned me in this terrible place. After a while I wouldn't
even go to the glass window to talk to her. I stayed angrily in my
bed, and when the nurse brought in my mother's gifts of oranges
and books, I made her leave them with the girl in the next bed
. . . until my mother was gone and I could claim them.

About four years later it was my mother who was scared,
lonely and unable to find the right words. The quarrels between
my father and her had grown louder and stormier, until finally she

packed up my brother and me and took us away to another apartment. "It's better this way," she told us. "You'll like your new school." She said little else about what had happened, partly because in my childish, grudging way I had made that glass partition a permanent piece of our life's furniture.

Beyond that, my mother could hardly expect an 11-year-old daughter to understand very much about the emotional strains and ambivalence that had led her to this step. Yet she must have been overwhelmed with anguish by her shattered marriage, and perhaps a bit ashamed too; hers was the first divorce in her family.

She must have been terrified as well at the prospect of now being the main support of two young children. There was little demand just then for a secretary who could take shorthand in three languages, none of them English. Finally she had to exchange those flowered, cotton housedresses that mothers used to wear for her first pair of slacks and a job at the Brooklyn Navy Yard. She learned to read ships' blueprints and to operate a giant crane—a remarkable skill for a woman who has never been able to pass a driver's test for a car.

My own emotional response to the divorce was one of relief at no longer having to hide in my room, hands over my ears, so as not to hear my parents quarreling. It was a monstrously selfish reaction, I thought secretly, and I was too filled with guilt to tell my mother. I was having trouble, too, making new friends in a strange neighborhood, and though I didn't want to worry my mother, she must have known about it. After being on her feet all week at work, she would spend Sundays with me, tramping through every museum in the city of New York.

Not long after the divorce, my father met and married a woman who had her own Jewish-language radio program. I didn't mention it to my new friends, since stepmothers were not a common commodity in our crowd, and I was somewhat embarrassed when mine began to use my father's last name on the air. I was not impressed with her glamour because my own mother had suddenly become a figure of high romance in my eyes.

At the back of a bottom drawer of an old and scratched bureau, hidden under piles of her underwear—the garments were always too warm and sensible ever to be called "lingerie"—I had discovered a slender, leather-bound volume of poems. I could make out my mother's name on the dedication, but that was all I could decipher of the mysterious, scrolled German lettering.

When I asked her about the book, I think my mother blushed. Then she told me that a long time ago in her small village in Czechoslovakia, the poems had been written about her and then published by a young man who had loved her. "Did you love him too?" I asked in a whisper. And for once in her life my mother answered me plainly. "Yes. Very much."

She explained that he was a councilman's son and she was but a grocer's daughter. It was a time and a place when young people did not defy their parents, and the romance ended when his family arranged a different, "more suitable" marriage for him. To help her forget, my mother's family sent her to the United States. She arrived carrying a sturdy suitcase bound with leather straps and filled with little of value except that book.

I looked at my mother with awe. She was a simple, modest, practical woman, devoted to hard work, balanced meals and galoshes when it looked like rain. She still spoke with a slight accent, dressed plainly, was unskilled at makeup and a stranger to the beauty parlor. Yet a young man once had created poetry out of her "mysterious eyes" and the way the sunlight looked on her "chestnut hair."

I don't remember much of what my mother translated for me from that book and I don't really care whether it was good poetry or just doggerel. I do know that I felt worse than ever about being so clumsily tall and about having braces on my teeth and such meanly straight hair. "No one will ever write a poem about me," I said. My mother, who was not much given to touching and hugging, cradled me in her arms then and, stroking my hair, assured me that I was wrong. "Someday," she promised. "Someday."

Such moments of real communication between us were rare. We left so many things unsaid, each of us half wishing, half daring the other to guess what was beneath the surface, and each of us being disappointed in turn.

I remember that my mother was too shy to talk about human

bodies or sex. When she thought the time had come, she wrote away for pamphlets that were supposed to explain everything a young girl should know about such things.

Later, when I won a flock of medals at high school graduation, I kept my silence. "There wasn't much competition," I said, shrugging away the triumph. I wanted my mother to disagree. I thought that somehow she should know how important I wanted them to be to *her*. Instead, I came home one day to find her using the medals as bright, shining things to amuse a visiting baby. Angrily I snatched them away, startling my mother and making the baby cry.

Even when my father divorced his second wife and began a second courtship of my mother, we kept our deeper thoughts to ourselves. When my parents announced they would be remarried, we talked about where we would live and what we would buy. My mother allowed me to go shopping with her for a trousseau and we filled her drawers with real lingerie for the first time. There was a small wedding in the apartment of a friend, but my brother and I were forbidden to attend. "It wouldn't look right," my mother told us. Instead, we went to a movie.

The second time around was no more a storybook marriage than the first, but my parents had learned a certain tolerance for each other's faults. They had come to realize that if they were not completely happy together, they were even less content apart, and they were better with each other now than they had been before.

I knew that the book of poems was still in my mother's bottom drawer. If my father ever came across it, during either of their marriages, he never said anything. A remembrance out of the dim past, the slim book was not what stood between my mother and my father, and it did not keep her from doing her wifely best. Still, when my father died, my mother must have felt guilty about it. Several months after the funeral, when I asked her about the book, she told me, "I burned it when Dad died." Then, before I could say anything else, she got very busy in the kitchen.

Many years after my mother promised it would happen, a young man did write a poem about me. Even better, he married me. We have our quarrels, of course, but he is a gentle, intuitive man who usually tells me what he is feeling and insists that I tell him.

I keep a copy of my husband's poem in a bottom drawer, in a brown accordion folder where I hoard all of life's vital documents—college diploma, passport, marriage license, a son's birth certificate. In that same folder I also treasure a letter from my mother.

We had disagreed about something—I no longer remember what. As usual, we had not shouted at each other and we also had not explained what each of us was really angry about. Instead we said our good-byes coolly, and a week passed without either of us calling the other. Then the letter arrived. "Please don't be angry," my mother wrote. "You know that I am not a demonstrative woman. I never say it, but I love you very much."

It means a great deal to me to have those words written out. My mother and I still speak through a glass partition most of the time. If she reads this article, she will tell me what a cousin or neighbor thinks about it instead of what it might mean to her. Still, that's all right now. While we still have many years to share together, we are slowly learning to understand each other's codes and to decipher the halting, roundabout ways we tell each other "I love you."

Claire Safran

"Be a Good Boy"

On August 18, 1920, Tennessee became the 36th state to ratify the 19th Amendment, providing the two-thirds majority of states needed to grant women the right to vote. The story of how a crucial vote came to be cast by a young legislator from the tiny Tennessee town of Niota is a wonderful illustration of how one mother changed the course of history.

Henry Thomas Burn, at 23 the youngest member of Tennessee's House of Representatives, was securely in the camp of the anti-suffragists—voting staunchly throughout a day of parliamentary maneuvering to table the measure rather than bring it to a vote. Like many of his legislative contemporaries, he endorsed the words of the anti-suffragist leader, Alice Wadsworth, that granting the vote to women would "enshrine nagging as a national policy."

A tie vote on a measure to table the amendment kept it alive. Its opponents decided to bring the issue to a vote on the floor of the House, reasoning that the same tie would defeat the amendment.

Unlike other opponents of the 19th Amendment, Mr. Burn had received a letter from his mother, Febb Ensminger Burn, which he carried that day in his pocket. In the letter, Mrs. Burn wrote to her son: "Hurry and vote for suffrage. Don't forget to be a good boy."

As voting began on the amendment, Mr. Burn surprised everyone in the chamber by switching his position and voting in favor of women's right to vote. He later explained his action in a speech from the floor. His most telling statement was: "I know that a mother's advice is safest for her boy to follow and my mother wanted me to vote for ratification."

On August 24, 1920, Tennessee Governor Albert H. Roberts signed the amendment, thus giving women throughout the nation the right to vote.

Jack Ryan

The Light Within

*It is better to light one candle
than curse the darkness.*

—Motto of the Christopher Society

How well I remember the days we spent in the doctor's office, and all the events leading up to those days. It began when Mom was well into her 70s, when her vision deteriorated noticeably. Over a period of several months, macular degeneration was diagnosed. Mom's world was shattered.

I remember how hungry we were for some good news every time we went to Dr. Greenburg's office, hoping against hope that he would see something through those powerful lenses that would contradict his previous diagnosis. Every time he placed her chin in that cup and peered deeply into her almost blind eyes, I sat in the examining room and silently prayed for a miracle. As I knew she did. For months on end, we heard, instead, even more bad news. The retina was detached, the vision was worsening, there was nothing more that could be done for her.

I would take her hand and lead her out of the doctor's office, and each time, she unfailingly would say a cheerful good-bye to the doctor and his staff. She would keep her composure, and say "thank you" to everyone with her customary gratitude for any thoughtful or solicitous acts. And, of course, everyone was most kind to this woman, who was by now well-known in that office for her amazing resilience.

We would leave each appointment shaken, upset and afraid to talk about what we were both thinking. I would try to be optimistic because the doctor never said she would never see anything again—not even the faintest shadows. Instead, he hoped as we did that she would retain some vision. So I would drive her home, guiding her every step, and not let her know my own eyes were blinded by tears of frustration and sadness for her.

Today she is 85 and has been totally blind for more than five years. Over the course of these past five years, something remarkable has taken the place of the anguish and despair I know she went through while waiting for that terrible curtain to fall. The remarkable thing is that when there were no longer any appointments because it was clear there would be no miracle and she was blind, she began to repeat what the doctor had been telling her for many months.

Remember, he would say, that you have seen your 12 children. You have seen them grow and marry and have children of their own. Think about how fortunate you have been, Ann, compared with those who are blind from birth or who lose their sight when they are young. Think of those less fortunate than you, he would say to her, when she cried bitter tears and had to let go of her hope.

Almost from the day the doctor said these words to my mother, she began to repeat them to anyone who asked about her condition. To all the expressions of sympathy and to all those who tried to comfort her, she would repeat what Dr. Greenburg said. To my astonishment, she began to believe these words. I saw her attitude change from despair and resentment to a quiet acceptance that is an inspiration to me to this day.

Even today, to anyone meeting her for the first time who expresses sympathy, she will say, "What's the point in complaining? After all, there are people worse off." As the years in darkness have passed, I've noticed that this response has become more assertive. In the beginning, it was tentative and tinged with self-pity. Now it's like a campaign theme, or a mantra that has given her the answer she needs to the unanswerable question of "Why me?"

Every day I think of her world of darkness, and of how she finds joy and purpose in her life despite her handicap. She has friends, books on tape, television programs she "watches" because she remembers what various people like Angela Lansbury on "Murder She Wrote" look like, and she conjures up that visual memory while she listens to their voices. She has love for and from her 10 surviving children and many grandchildren— and remembers every birthday, anniversary and date and time of every last phone call, from New York to California.

She has grace and courage and spirit, and I love her deeply for all she has taught me. Most of all, I thank her for teaching me to count my blessings. I don't know whether or not she feels in her heart that she is more fortunate than many others who have never seen a sunrise or their children's faces, but she *acts* as though she believes it. Maybe that's what really counts. In forcing herself to accept her blindness, she has come to a peaceful, true acceptance.

Every evening, when I call to tell her what's on the television set that she can't see but nevertheless eagerly tunes into, she says, "I love you, Diane." And I say, "I love you, too, Mom." And that says it all.

Diane DeLeo

With a Little Help from Mama

To dream of the person you would like to be is to waste the person you are.

—Unknown

It was a beautiful spring morning when Mama and I set off from our ranch in Oklahoma for Nashville, Tennessee, where I was going to audition for a recording contract. I was 20 years old, well prepared vocally, ready to take a chance on the dream of a lifetime.

But as the hillsides rolled by, resplendent with the whites and pinks of dogwood and redbud blossoms, I felt a creeping uneasiness. The closer we got to the country music capital, the more I tried to prolong the trip, making Mama detour for some sightseeing, then for a snack, then for anything I could think of. Finally, I yelled "Stop" and Mama pulled the big blue Ford into a Dairy Queen on the side of the highway and we went inside.

As I toyed with my mountain of ice cream, I didn't have to explain I was scared. Mama knew me too well. "Reba Nell," she said, adding the Nell for gentle emphasis, "we can turn around right now and go on back home if that's what you want, and I'll understand. The music business is not for everyone."

I looked at Mama across the melting swirl of my sundae. She

wasn't pushing me. But when she was my age Mama would have given just about anything to have had the opportunity I was getting a chance at now. I wondered if that was what was confusing me.

We'd always had a special bond. Maybe it was because of my singing. Music had gone way back in Mama's life. But right out of high school she had to take a teaching job, working in a two-room schoolhouse. Then she married, worked as an assistant to the school superintendent, and did all the bookkeeping on our ranch while raising four kids.

Mama and I were middle kids, both the third of four children. Being a middle kid, I was always looking for attention. I was a tomboy, doing everything my older brother, Pake, did. "Anything you can do I can do better!" was our sibling motto. Whether it was throwing rocks and doing chin-ups, or riding horses and roping, I was out to be the best, to get the attention. Then I learned to sing.

I remember in the second grade my music teacher, pretty Mrs. Kanton, helped me learn "My Favorite Things" from *The Sound of Music*. When I went home and sang it for Mama, her eyes met mine and just sort of glowed. It tickled me to think I could make Mama react like that, and to hear adults say I was gifted.

That's what my grandmother—Mama's mother and my namesake—used to say when I was growing up. But she called it a special gift, a gift from God. I was almost as close to her as I was to Mama. Grandma used to take me fishing at a pond on her place. We never did catch much, but we liked to throw in our lines and sit on the pond dam while Grandma told stories, mostly from the Bible. She told me about David, Moses and Daniel, and the special gifts that God had given them, like courage and leadership and prophecy. In fact, David was a songwriter.

I probably learned as much of my Bible going fishing with Grandma as I did in Sunday school. She taught me gospel songs and hymns so I could sing to her. "Reba," she'd say, "God gives us all our own special gifts, and he's given you yours for a reason. Now you have to learn to use it."

The cherry was sliding down the whipped cream peak on my sundae. I looked outside at the glowing Dairy Queen cone rotating slowly, almost as if it were sitting on a record turntable. Mama was nursing a cup of coffee and watching the traffic flash by. She was not about to rush me.

We'd spent many an hour on the road together. Grandpap and Daddy were champion steer ropers. Summers we'd all go with Daddy on the rodeo circuit. We had a two-horse trailer that was so heavy, all four of us kids had to stand on the back of it so Daddy could pull the nose up and hitch it to the Ford. Then we'd pile into the back seat and take off for rodeos in Wyoming and Colorado. We'd play road games, like counting mile markers or Volkswagens. We'd see who could spot the most out-of-state license plates.

Then someone struck up a song and everybody joined in. Mama coached. She kept us on pitch and taught us how to harmonize. If the lyrics got lost in the jumble, she announced, "Okay, stop. Reba Nell, *enunciate.* Now go ahead." One word would do it. That was the schoolteacher coming out in her.

When we got older, Pake, my younger sister, Susie, and I formed a country-and-western band at Kiowa High School. We called ourselves the Singing McEntires. We practiced in the living room while Mama was in the kitchen frying potatoes. I remember one day we were singing harmonies and things got a little messed up. I was on Susie's part or Susie was on Pake's—we couldn't tell—but Pake got really aggravated and started bossing us around. Quick enough, Mama marched in, spatula in hand. "All right," she said, "sing it."

We sang it.

"Susie, you're on Reba's part," she said, pointing with her spatula. "Now, just sing the song." We sang it.

"That sounds better. Sing it again." We sang it again.

"That's perfect. Now do it once more." Then she walked back into the kitchen. That was Mama.

Across the Formica tabletop I caught Mama glancing at her watch. I couldn't stall much longer. My ice cream had turned to soup.

After my voice had matured into a real singer's instrument, I started performing at rodeos. I loved singing to the big crowds. I'd listen to my favorite country music stars, like Loretta Lynn and

Dolly Parton, and go out there and try to sound just like them and get all that attention. Then one day Mama took me aside for a quiet talk that would turn out to be one of the most important conversations we ever had.

"Reba Nell," she said, "you have a beautiful voice all your own. If people want to hear Dolly or Loretta sing, they'll buy their albums. But now you've got to find your own style. Sing what you feel, sing from your own heart, and you'll discover the voice God intended for you. That's what people will really come to hear."

She was right. After our talk, people in the music business started taking a real look at me, and that's why we were now sitting her in this Dairy Queen outside Nashville.

I looked up at Mama. She was fishing in her purse for the keys to the Ford.

"Reba," she said, pulling them out, "I'm serious about turning back. But if you get that record deal, I'll be very proud of you. If you don't—I'll be just as proud." Then she reached over and gave me a tight hug, and suddenly I remembered the glow in her eyes when I sang "My Favorite Things."

I knew what that glow had meant. All Mama wanted—all any mother wants for her child—was for me to be myself. And she'd seen what I could be. She didn't have to say that if I signed a record deal she'd be living out her dreams a little bit through me. I understood that now and I was proud. Suddenly I wanted to get to Nashville as quick as we could.

And I've been making records ever since, using those gifts that Grandma talked about and Mama helped me find. The gifts God provides to make each of us unique.

Reba McEntire

The Mother Who Teed It Up
—and Taught Life

*The reasonable thing is to learn
from those who can teach.*

—Sophocles

I would guess that very few children got their inspirations for life from their mother's golf game. But then, they didn't know my mother. Golf was my mother's milk. On the links, one learned how to become a gentleman or a lady.

My mother's theory was that if you couldn't trust a golfer on the links, you surely couldn't trust him or her anywhere. If he or she didn't keep score properly, moved the ball ever so slightly in the rough, or used a "hand mashie" (throwing the ball without being seen), the jig was up. Not to be trusted.

At an early age, eight or nine, I was drafted along with my sister to caddie for the Old Lady (as we called my mother behind her back), who was then in her mid-30s. It was a dual purpose: (1) to save money by not using one of the club's caddies; but more important, (2) to teach us the rules of life. So out we would go for a morning stroll, lugging a heavy set of golf clubs and listening to the lessons of life. (Father would stay home to read the newspapers.) She permitted us to chase what few balls she would hit in the woods, thus avoiding poison ivy for herself, which

50

taught us how to spot the shiny leaf and avoid it like the itch. This was a toughening process, one of many our golfing parent taught us.

Swearing, of course, was forbidden—we could not use the name of the Lord in vain or any one of a number of phrases we heard frequently on the links. When we got home, of course, we immediately made for the telephone to share the forbidden phrases with our friends. (Yes, they had phones way back then.)

Self-control and silence were also great lessons to be learned: Don't talk while the ball is in play. For kids, a game almost requires cheering if their side is winning, so when mother hit a good shot or putted into the cup, our instincts naturally called for a cheer. Not on the golf course, we were warned. Poor sportsmanship against the opponent, impolite and unacceptable. Another lesson in preparing two youngsters for the niceties of life.

And so it went. These lessons might as well have been carved in stone, so immutable were they. And great lessons they were, too. Both my sister and I learned right from wrong, and how to behave toward other people. And while it was the golf course where these commandments were taught, they have lasted in all our endeavors for the more than 70 years that we have been around.

Good work, Mother. Thanks for the lessons. Without them, we would be out of bounds all the time.

Allan H. Kalmus

"Your Time Is Coming"

*Be strong and of good courage; be not afraid,
neither be thou dismayed; for the Lord thy God
is with thee whithersoever thou goest.*

—Joshua 1:9

That day in March 1991 seemed so unreal. Until then my mind
had been all wrapped up in football for more than six months.
Only weeks earlier I'd had one of the greatest thrills of my life:
The New York Giants had won Super Bowl XXV. After six-and-a-
half frustrating years in the National Football League, mostly sitting on the bench, I'd achieved my goal. I'd been the starting, the
winning, quarterback. That was real. But not this. . . .

I'd come back to the old farmhouse where I grew up, near
Holsopple in western Pennsylvania. Flowers were everywhere.
Through misty eyes I glanced at the tear-stained faces of my dad
and my brothers and sisters. We clung to one another. Friends
and relatives drifted in and out. I heard quiet words of consola-
tion, accepted comforting hugs, felt pain deep inside. Yet I kept
hoping that at any moment I might wake up and discover this
was all a bad dream. It wasn't. Suddenly Mom was gone. I'd
known of the terrible pain she suffered from arthritis and back
problems that had required several surgeries, but I hadn't been
prepared for this.

One of my sisters found Mom's diary—actually a spiral-bound

notebook in which she had recorded the happenings of the day as well as her conversations with God. "There's a lot about you in here," my sister said. "I think you should read it." She knew how much I'd depended on Mom's encouragement over the years.

I took the diary into the family room, sat down and began to read. And remember. . . .

"Remember Whose you are," Mom had often told me. "God has a special plan for your life." She filled us kids' minds with Scripture—even taped Bible verses to the refrigerator so we'd have to read them before breakfast. There were times, however, when I was sure God had either shelved the plan for *my* life or He was looking the other way.

Like the time I was recruited as a quarterback by Penn State. I got to play in a few games, but Coach Joe Paterno had another quarterback, Todd Blackledge, whom he elected to keep as his starter. In order to become a starter, I transferred to West Virginia University.

Then, after two good years at West Virginia, including two Bowl games, I was drafted in 1984 by the New York Giants. I thought at the time, *At last, God's plan is finally settling into place.* However, that move to the Giants only led to another time of testing. I knew I would have to spend a certain period on the bench, learning from the older quarterbacks such as starter Phil Simms. But after five years, I was getting tired of sitting on the bench when I knew I could do the job out on the field.

How hard it was, pacing up and down the sidelines, game after game, season after season, toting my little clipboard as if I were playing a board game, watching every move on the field, analyzing every play, both ours and the opposing team's. After a while I was able to read the plays so well that I could often predict what the other team was going to do just by the way the players were lining up. But from the sidelines I could do nothing.

Meanwhile, Mom was saying, "Your time is coming. Be patient. Remember, God still has a special plan for your life." My head wanted to agree with her, but in my bones I didn't feel it—especially knowing that Mom had to endure her own pain. Then my wife, Vicky, and I had our first child. Jason was born with heart complications. He required four major operations before he was 11 months old. Where was God's plan in that? I wondered. But Mom helped us pray through that time, and Jason is alive and well today. I'm sure it was because of all those prayers.

My first real chance as a pro quarterback came in the fall of 1988, my fifth season with the Giants. In week 12, Phil Simms got hurt. The following week I was given the start against the New Orleans Saints: my big chance to prove myself—or so I thought.

For most of the first half, the coaches gave us one running play after another. Our team was known for running the ball on the first down, but now we also were running on second and third. About the only time I was allowed to throw was when we were third and long. Then on one of those plays, I spotted Stephen Baker downfield in the open and heaved a pass at him. Stephen took off, dodging one tackler after another, and scored. It was an 85-yard pass play, the longest for the Giants since 1972.

By halftime, even though we were down 9-7 because of the Saints' three field goals, I felt we were really beginning to move. The coaches were letting me loosen up, not running the ball all the time. I connected with five out of 10 passes for 128 yards and no interceptions. As the half ended, I trotted into the locker room, adrenaline still pumping as I anticipated an even better second half.

Imagine my shock, then, when Coach Bill Parcells walked over to me before the second half. "I'm going to make a move here," he said, indicating that he was planning to put in backup quarterback Jeff Rutledge. "You played a great first half, and if things don't go well, you're going right back in." As I walked out to the sidelines, I was in a state of shock. We won the game on a field goal, but I was too upset to enjoy it.

"Parcells just lost me as a player," I complained in the locker room to sportswriters, who were only too happy for a little controversy. I called my agent and demanded to be traded. But management wouldn't go for it.

Later Mom tried to encourage me. "Just because things aren't going your way doesn't mean God's plan has changed. Don't give up."

Well, I didn't give up. I looked down at Mom's diary again,

finding those same words written, and then her prayer asking God to give me His peace, asking Him to help me stick it out. Asking Him to give me a chance—when the time was right.

It seemed to take forever, but that chance to prove myself finally came in 1990, my seventh season with the Giants. Once again Simms went down, this time with a season-ending injury, and I went in. For six-and-a-half years I had been memorizing our offensive plays and analyzing our opponents' defenses. Now I would have to lead the team for the rest of the season and into the playoffs, hoping to make it to the Super Bowl.

We finished the regular season by beating the Phoenix Cardinals, 24-21, and the New England Patriots, 13-10. Next, in the playoffs, we clobbered the Chicago Bears 31-3 and set our sights on the seemingly invincible San Francisco 49ers.

I turned the page in Mom's diary. She'd wanted so much to be at the game, but she was too sick to make the trip to the West Coast. So she planted her pain-racked body in front of the television set and watched me play one of the biggest games of my life. She kept notes of everything—all my statistics, the words of the television sports announcers, her emotions during the knockdown, drag-out game in which 49er quarterback Joe Montana was flattened.

Mom's notes on the game brought it all back. There we were in the fourth quarter, down by four points. We hadn't been able to score a touchdown, only three field goals. I was dropping back to pass, focusing on our wide receivers downfield, when out of the corner of my eye I glimpsed a flash of red and gold. It was too late to move out of the way. In an instant Jim Burt crashed into my leg with the force of what seemed like a freight train. Pain such as I had never felt before seared through my leg and shot through my body, all the way to my head. I dropped to the ground, writhing. At that moment I was sure it was all over; I was finished.

I glanced down at the page in Mom's diary. My eyes riveted on the short, emotion-filled sentences she'd written: "Oh God, stoop down and heal my son. Replace his pain with peace. Let him finish the game he's waited so many years to play. . . ."

And I remembered—3,000 miles away I lay on the field as the trainers gathered around me. The pain was brutal. Fear rose up within me.

Then suddenly everything seemed to stop. A calming, peaceful sensation started at the top of my head, eased its way down through my body, through my leg, right down to my toes. The pain and fear faded. I knew I could get up, and I did, walking off the field under my own power.

Of course everybody, especially Coach Parcells, was worried. Three times he came to me and asked, "Hoss, can you go back in?" Twice I answered, "Yeah, I can go," and the final time I said, "Bill, I'm going."

We got a fourth field goal. Finally, behind by one point, with only two-and-a-half minutes left to play and the ball on our own 43-yard line, I drilled a pass to Mark Bavaro for 19 yards, then one to Stephen Baker for 13. With virtually no time left on the clock, we were in field-goal range. Matt Bahr booted a heart-stopping kick that won the game, 15-13, and gave us our spot opposite the Buffalo Bills in the Super Bowl.

I looked again at the diary, tears in my eyes. Never had I imagined the intensity of Mom's prayers. No wonder she could say with confidence, "Remember Whose you are. God has a special plan for your life." Despite her own pain, she enjoyed an intimacy with God that had allowed her to make her request with boldness and certainty. I had been healed, restored and strengthened. Because of her prayer, I was enabled to go on and lead our team to victory there, and later in Super Bowl XXV.

Mom's no longer here to remind me that I belong to God, and that He has a special plan for my life. But I believe it now, without any doubt. It's true. Maybe not a plan to win all the time, or to be spared trouble and pain. But a plan for me to be strong and persevere. Mom has achieved her goal.

Jeff Hostetler

Parents Say
the Darndest Things

The Miami Herald reported the following actual written excuses given to teachers in Albuquerque, New Mexico, by moms (and dads) explaining a child's absence from school:

"Please excuse Blanche from jim today. She is administrating."

"Please excuse John from being absent on Jan. 28, 29, 30, 31, 32 and also 33."

"Excuse Gloria. She has been under the doctor."

"Please excuse Johnnie for being. It was his father's fault."

"My daughter was absent yesterday because she was tired. She spent the weekend with the Marines."

"Please excuse Sara for being absent. She was sick and I had her shot."

"Carlos was absent because he was playing football. He was hit in the growing part."

"Please excuse Ray Friday from school. He has very loose vowels."

Gifts My Mother Gave Me

The mother's heart is the child's schoolroom.

—Henry Ward Beecher

I can remember winter mornings before there were words, when I awoke to a backyard transformed into a foreign landscape under drifts of fresh show, the branches of the elms hanging low with ice. The world was never so quiet as on those mornings; even the squirrels looked surprised.

The next thing I remember is the first purple crocus suddenly appearing in the snow outside the kitchen window. It was a message that spring was coming.

I remember how the earth looked as the last snow melted; the smell of lily of the valley; the snowball bushes luminous on spring nights. As I watched my mother cross-pollinate roses with a clean paint brush, I learned about the ministrations of the bees, who in their rush for pollen leave dusty footprints behind.

I remember tasting colors before I knew their names: pink, lilac, cerulean blue.

I remember feeling sculpture before I learned to look at it. On my first visit to a museum, I ran up to the bust of a young boy and ran my hands along its contours. My mother and a museum guard watched and smiled because they understood it was a child's way of learning the language of space.

Then there were words, and my first book, which my mother wrote and illustrated, about an elf-man who lived in a grand piano and emerged to perform small feats of magic. The performer of magic, of course, was my mother, my first and finest teacher. She showed me how to be still: to see, to hear and to feel the magic animus in every living thing.

It wasn't only nature she transformed. At a tiny branch library she introduced me to books. Learning to read was no chore. How miraculous that a human being, long after death, could reach across the years and conjure in a reader's head images, tears and laughter. She taught me about the music in language so that I could watch Olivier's Richard III, understanding nothing of the plot, but so spellbound that for some time thereafter I wrote only in unrhymed iambic pentameter.

Because life was sacred, every stray cat found shelter in our home. I remember the newborn kitten my mother brought to my bed one morning. I buried my nose in its warm fur and smelled the sweet smell of tentative life. I smelled it again 20 years later, when a beloved poodle lay dying in my arms. Perhaps it is the smell of eternity, lingering briefly after we enter this world, returning to signal our voyage home.

First my mother gave me life; then she gave me to life, orienting me positively to myself, to nature and to human beings.

It is no accident that in many cultures the word for priest and teacher is the same, or that initially the sole purpose of higher education was training for the clergy. Education is inherently moral, teaching a profoundly religious act. For at the heart of my mother's magic, as with any great lesson, lay belief in the divinity of nature, in the integrity of creatures smaller than ourselves, in the awesomeness of mysteries. To discover a physical or mathematical law is to understand the symmetry of God. To fall under the spell of literature is to be enchanted by the divine magic of creation. Remember your own best teachers: did they not give you this same gift? In celebrating the wonder and the goodness of the world, they gave you to life.

My mother died last summer. When we meet again, it will be as two souls so intertwined it is impossible to tell where one stops and the other starts. For, as our forbears understood, the primary function of a teacher is to touch another human being's soul and, in doing so, to turn it irrevocably to the light.

Dona M. Kagan

Golden Friendships

I have learned that to have a good friend is the purest of all God's gifts, for it is a love that has no exchange of payment.

—Frances Farmer

Mom's closest friends are either still "up North" in New York—as we say in South Florida—or they have died. In a few cases, her old friends are now women whose mental functions are impaired by senility and it can be heartbreaking to listen in when she occasionally calls one of them. Since she hasn't mastered the system blind people use for locating numbers on the phone, these calls are usually placed for her with a good deal of prior discussion.

These contacts are so important to her, I'll know a week in advance that I need to place a call for her at precisely three o'clock the following Sunday, and she will remember exactly when she last called Betty or Evelyn, or whoever it may be. On a good day, her old friend will be responsive, but often I'll hear her say things like "Don't you remember? I've moved to Florida!" or she will repeat her phone number a dozen times because, once again, it's been misplaced. Unlike Mom, who remembers phone numbers, birthdays, anniversaries and other vital information, her friend needs to be reminded.

They talk about the same things every time. The weather, their health, the comings and goings of their children and grandchildren.

It doesn't matter if they talked a month or a year ago, the subjects hardly ever vary. This is the stuff and substance of their lives and no detail is too small.

Listening to Mom talk to her friends—even the ones who can't remember where she lives—is a lesson for me in what real friendship is all about. First of all, it's about caring what happens to people, no matter how tough your own life may be. Listening to a blind 85-year-old woman whose hearing isn't what it used to be commiserating with a friend who can't remember things is a real lesson in caring. It makes me feel ashamed that I often don't call friends because I'm down in the dumps or too busy or for a million other reasons. Being a friend means constancy. It means you call even when you don't feel like it, because friendship is often about doing something for someone else.

I forgot how much friendship is also about loyalty. We went to one of the local shopping malls recently where Mom ran into two women who live in her development. She didn't see them, of course, but they recognized her and greeted her effusively. It was just a brief exchange, during which she introduced me, and they were on their way.

"What phony baloney," she said excitedly when they were well ahead of us. Since the remark came from nowhere, I asked her what she meant. With obvious disdain, she explained that she has sat under the canopy at her pool on several occasions with these two women and one of their friends, Sylvia. One day, she said, she sat nearby and heard the three of them talking about the wedding reception of Sylvia's daughter the week before. They raved about the food, the flowers, the elegant country club location and the beautiful bride. Mom said Sylvia was obviously beaming with pride, and delighted to hear from her close friends, once more, what every mother likes to hear when her daughter marries.

"Well, then Sylvia left, and you should have heard them," Mom said as I guided her towards the mall exit. "I couldn't believe friends could be that two-faced. They ripped her apart, talking about how cheap she was, her homely son-in-law, the music they couldn't dance to. It was awful. And they call themselves friends," she clucked. "Who needs friends like that?"

I don't think I'd do that to a friend, Mom, but you do remind me of the times I'm tempted to disparage another woman so I can gain some advantage. It's usually a business situation because we all know it's a dog-eat-dog world out there and women don't behave any more decently than men. At least, that's been my experience. But I'm glad to say that my better nature prevails and if I have a friend—a coworker or anyone else—I try to be loyal.

Maybe that's a lesson I learned from my mother a long time ago, and there's something ingrained because being disloyal to a friend—and I've done it—makes me very uncomfortable. I don't mean any major breach of friendship, like divulging a confidence when you're sworn to secrecy, but small acts of betrayal. In a competitive situation in the office, for example, where politics reign no matter the size or nature of the organization. There have been times I've subtly undermined a friend who might be competing with me for a new assignment, promotion or whatever the prize.

This kind of rivalry would be hard for Mom to grasp. Her idea of competing with friends is rooted in her experience as a home-maker. She comes from the era when women really did worry about someone seeing spots on their imperfectly washed glasses, or the boys I dated in high school were rated according to whether or not their shirts were brilliant white or dingy gray. She comes from an era and from a world where her friends were a cadre of like-minded, extraordinarily focused women who were the best wives and mothers they could be. I remember that group of Mom's friends as though they were an elite women's club. Not everybody could join, and once you were accepted as a member, you were a member for life.

Mom was probably unofficial president of "the club" because of her unchallenged position as SuperMom. I was about 10 years old when we moved from the Lower East Side of Manhattan to East 77th Street—now the fashionable Upper East Side. It wasn't fash-ionable in those days when it was known as Yorkville, home of a large German, Polish and Irish population. But it was New York City during the fabled days of the "melting pot," when the city was a safe, vibrant place with clean streets and even middle-class people could afford apartments with fireplaces and elevators.

In those days, in the early 50s, the streets were safe enough that some of us slept on the fire escape on hot summer nights and, in the early evening, Mom and her friends would congregate on the "stoop" of our five-story walk-up. (We weren't part of the middle class that could afford fireplaces and elevators). I don't know what they found to talk about in the evening, because they had also been together most of the day in the park at the end of our street. Every day, they occupied the same two benches just inside the park's entrance. Baby carriages, bicycles and shopping bags with sandwiches, fruit and cold drinks formed a barricade around them, like the moat in front of a castle and they were, indeed, like royalty in the way they behaved.

It wasn't anything overt, but when I approached my mother's bench, I knew Mom, Evelyn, Betty, Marie, and the others occupied some rarefied position in that world. Walking the few short blocks from PS 158 on York Avenue and 77th Street to John Jay Park, I was certain that my mother would be on her bench, with my newborn baby brother or sister in the carriage near her (there was a new one every year) and that all the other mothers in the park knew that was my mother's place, every day. She and her friends were a privileged group that absolutely nobody tried to mess with.

Mom would proudly hold court as her school-age children came to her throne-like bench each day after school. Besides checking in with Mom before going home to change into play-clothes, it was understood that part of the ritual was a thorough inspection by Mom's friends. Although the inspection was friendly, I always felt like they were checking to be sure my middy blouse was snowy white and starched, and that the rest of me met their high standards.

Being clean was the highest virtue to these women, including my mother. Anyone whose windows were dirty in a neighborhood where women sat on window sills to wash their own windows, or whose laundry was dirty, in the days when laundry was hung from lines outside the back window and could be observed by all the neighbors, was not only a bad wife and mother but a seriously flawed human being. Horrified at evidence of dirt somewhere, they would say things like "there's no excuse for it—soap and water are cheap." Or, if someone showed signs of being spectacularly clean, they'd say things like "she's so clean you could eat off her floor."

Cleanliness was only one of the values these women shared. The others were all related to the same impulse that drove the passion for cleanliness—the need to nurture and protect home and family. Thus, men who were good providers were praised. Women who sacrificed for their children—as my mother did—were honored. Children who showed respect and love for their parents were adored and admired by all. There were other reasons people were either good or bad, of course, but these were the basic rules my mother and her friends lived by.

Those rules have changed enormously in the 50 years since Mom and her friends held court in John Jay Park. It's harder for women to bind together as wives and mothers because we no longer live in the same place for 20 years, as Mom and her friends did. Much is lost when we don't share the dailiness of life, year after year, from the small details like what's the price of hamburger today to the major events on every human calendar, from birth to death. And women are not home the way they were 50 years ago. They are out in the workplace in large numbers struggling to balance the needs of family and their responsibilities to an employer.

There are also many isolating influences in modern life that make it difficult to remain close to friends—or even family members. The automobile, shopping mall, TV, suburban sprawl and urban blight all contribute to keeping us apart. The women who gather on the stoop, the front porch or in the back yard every day at an appointed time and spend hours together are a vanishing breed.

I don't for a moment wish we could all go back 50 years. Nor do I think that what ails America is the demise of family. There's no such thing as "the family." There are only individual families, some happy and many desperately unhappy. But I do look back on those days when Mom sat in the park with her friends as happy times, and sometimes I regret life isn't like that any more.

I regret that my daughter didn't have that same experience of knowing, with absolute certainty, that her mom would be in the park with all the other mommies every day. My daughter, instead, was taken to the park by a caring nanny, while I went to work. Of course, the nannies and nursemaids eventually all formed cliques and sat on their own benches. But it wasn't the same as those women of East 77th Street who owned the territory for themselves and for their children. Seeing Mom and her friends in the park every day made me feel all was right with the world.

For Mom, it doesn't matter how much the world or their lives have changed. The immutable laws of friendship still hold. That means caring, constancy and loyalty. It means, as Polonius urged Laertes in Hamlet "The friends thou hast, and their adoption tried, Grapple them to thy soul with hoops of steel." Mom probably never heard those words, but she and her friends know what it's all about. In fact, they probably have a patent on that particular steel.

Joan Aho Ryan

Memories of Minnie

Three things in human life are important:
The first is to be kind. The second is to be kind.
And the third is to be kind.

—Henry James

Mother's precepts were simple:

Love one another.
Help one another.
Use your head to save your heels.
Do not swear, dear.
Chew your gum with your mouth closed and lips together.
Be on time.
Obey your teacher.
Do not take what does not belong to you.
Don't be critical of others.
Remember "please" and "thank you."

Born in 1873 in Evanston, Illinois, my mother, Minnie Peterson, was a petite, gentle lady who was also strong and vigorous. She lived to 93 years of age. She was a good cook and housekeeper, ironing by hand all the white ruffled curtains at the windows of our three-story house.

On Sundays she baked pies or cakes, but during the week dessert was a dish of applesauce or sliced bananas. ("Slice them thin, dear," she would remind my two sisters and me). Dessert was served only after we cleaned our plates. We were expected to sit with hands folded and to be quiet while waiting for dessert. We did not leave the table without permission. We helped with the dishes after meals and had fun, singing. The sisters washed the dishes while our brother helped to dry or put away.

Mother's main interests were family, church and membership in the Women's Christian Temperance Union, which was head-quartered in Evanston. Mother neither drank nor smoked nor swore. Her strongest expletives were "Oh, pshaw," or, when truly exasperated, "Mortals!" We were reprimanded, always quietly and gently, for saying "darn." We were allowed no fizzy drinks, like root beer or "Green River."

Serious and ready to meet adversity head-on, Mother was a remarkable lady. Her schooling was limited, but she was wise and strong and patient and loving toward all. I never heard her make an unkind or hateful statement about anyone.

I am grateful to her for my inheritance of good hair, good skin—and honesty.

Evelyn B. Secrist

On the Way to Holy Ireland

*I am not afraid of storms, for I am
learning how to sail my ship.*

—Louisa May Alcott

Mom had just turned 70 and was living alone in a good-sized house in northwest Washington, D.C. Dad had been dead about five years. Living alone didn't bother her. She was independent and of good spirit. She kept up a lively telephone connection with my brother Neil and me, both bachelors living in New York, and she visited us fairly often.

There was the time we met her at the Port Authority Bus Terminal, where she was arriving for a major party, and she asked for help with a large canvas-on-wheels shopping bag. It turned out to contain a case of Ballantine Scotch Whiskey, my mother's contribution to the party. As she explained, there were no taxes on it in Washington, so it was much less expensive than buying it in New York. She herself didn't drink—yet—but she was hospitable to friends who did. But that's another story.

She liked company. She grew up as one of 12 children, and was at peak exhilaration surrounded by people having a good time. Having company was Mom's high.

Mom's other passion was Ireland. Her grandmother had immigrated to America shortly before her own brother was imprisoned. It was an honorable charge, treason, a felony for smuggling

69

guns to Irish rebels during the British occupation. Naturally, he was a hero in Ireland and inspired even more fierce patriotism in his family.

I phoned Mother one day and said, "I've met a delightful Irish priest, Father Larry Higgins, here in New York. He just arrived from visiting his family in Ireland. He's on his way back to his parish in Florida, and plans to stop over in Washington to see friends. I told him, 'Stay at Mother's house. Neil and I will drive you down.' Invite your friends over." For my mother, this message was like the bell to the fire house.

Probably eight or ten of us sat around the living room that evening, fed and sipping, exchanging merry stories, Father Larry reporting on the Old Country and Mother interrogating him in depth.

At a pause, Mom announced, "I've always wanted to go to Ireland." Father Larry said, "Why don't you?" Mom chuckled, saying something about if they ever built a bridge . . . Father Larry said, "Why don't you just fly over?"

Now, Mother was 10 years old when the Wright brothers first flew. She and her brother and sisters grew up when the dazzling and daring transportation innovation was the motorcar. They regarded flying almost exactly as my generation did space travel. Lindbergh flew. Amelia Earhart flew. Barnstormers and death-defiers flew. *Ordinary* people didn't fly. Airports were where people went the occasional Sunday after Mass to watch airplanes take off and land. But Mom, fly? It never crossed the minds of mother's family, or of a large part of that generation.

So when Father Larry said why didn't she fly over, Mother smiled and said, "Oh, Father, I could never fly." He said, "But you want to go so badly." She said, "Yes, but I'm afraid to fly."

I joined the effort. "I've been to Ireland, and met the cousins you'd love to meet. And since I work for Pan American World Airways and don't have a wife, I can get you a 90 percent fare discount. Being a real sport, I'll even pay the 10 percent. You can fly free."

Father Larry pressed on. "Mrs. Burns, it's not like it used to be in the propeller planes. They were terrible; they took 13 hours and bumped all over the sky. Now with the jets, it's a mere five or so hours, and it's smooth and comfortable."

Mother laughed and said it was not the time or the comfort or the cost. "It's the fear of death if I fly in an airplane."

That gave the rooting section pause, but only briefly. Father Larry thought for a moment, then looked up and said, "Kathleen, you told us a bit ago that you're 70 years of age. How long have you got to go, anyway? What happier death could you hope for, than to die on your way to Holy Ireland?"

The room broke up in laughter, and hilarity resumed and continued into the night.

When I came downstairs in the morning, Mom was already in the kitchen, putting the coffee on. As the coffee perked I reviewed last night's fun, but she seemed distracted. She turned and looked at me and said, "How long have I got to go, anyway?"

Three months later, Mother, Neil and I took off on Pan Am to Ireland. The DC-8 took off at 9 o'clock at night with a light passenger load. She was scared but determined. When we started racing down the runway she squeezed her eyes shut and her fingernails, clutching Neil's and my hands from her seat between us, nearly drew blood. Eventually, eyes still clenched, she muttered, "Tell me when we've taken off."

"We took off about five minutes ago."

Her eyes popped open. "We did?" She looked around. We hadn't crashed, she was safe. She resumed breathing. She looked at Neil and me and grinned. She was a flier.

But this was not to be a routine flight. When we leveled off, Neil and I pulled up the armrests to make three seats into a bed for Mom, who soon fell asleep. Several hours into the flight, with most passengers sleeping, the purser, who knew I was a fellow Pan Am employee, told me that a navigational device had failed, and the airplane was making a gentle, unobtrusive turn back to Kennedy Airport.

Neil and I looked at each other. After 70 years of mistrusting airplanes, the first time she got into one, something went wrong. She'd never fly again.

Pan Am put us up in the Kennedy Airport Hotel. We left a

wakeup call to catch the 10 A.M. flight to London, which would divert to Shannon to drop off the passengers from last night's aborted flight.

Mom's wakeup call came before the hotel's. "I'm in the coffee shop; where are you two?" We hustled to join her. She said, "Wasn't that wonderful? They had a problem, and instead of taking a chance, they turned around and came back. Hurry up, we don't want to be late for the flight."

The trip surpassed her dreams. She met cousins she'd only heard of and they hit it off beautifully. She visited music pubs, saw the lakes of Killarney, visited the graveyard in her ancestral County Mayo parish.

She flew twice again to Ireland, the last time remaining by herself and flying home alone. She flew to Paris and to Puerto Rico. She flew the shuttle between Washington and New York. She flew to Tampa for the 25th anniversary of Father Larry's ordination.

Her brothers and sisters couldn't get over their elder sister's bravery. They came to see her off on flights. Just imagine! Kathleen *flies!* Incredible! She became a celebrity in her family.

Another test remained. When mother was well into her 70s, I learned to fly. Private pilot, single-engine land. Mom and I took the airline to Daytona and stayed with friends. From there, I wanted to fly her in a single-engine airplane to visit Miami Beach, where she and Dad got married and weathered the great hurricane of 1926. She wanted to, but . . .

This was altogether different. An airliner is a living room with windows too small to see outside and invisible pilots, all of whom are supermen. A small airplane is more like sitting 6,000 feet up in the air in wraparound glass, staring at the entire universe outside and strange levers and gauges inside. And when the pilot is somebody whose shortcomings you've known since you changed his diapers . . . But, she did it anyway.

Mother flew with me not because she wanted to, but because I was her son.

I have a picture of her getting into the Cessna 172, her expression pained but brave. I gave her my flight plan, showing the points we'd fly over, and the approximate times between them. I handed her my watch and said, "You mark the times we reach each point."

It was the first time Mother took off with her eyes closed since that first DC-8 flight. She clutched the pad with the flight log. Climbing out, I said, "See Daytona Raceway below?" But she didn't open her eyes.

Then I asked, "Did you record our takeoff time?" Her eyes popped open, and she said no. I told her the takeoff time and said, "When do we get to our first checkpoint?" She wrote down the takeoff time, added the time to the checkpoint and told me. I flew and she watched the watch. Ten minutes later she said, "We should be over the New Smyrna Beach airport." With an air of great authority, she looked below for the airport.

I said, "There it is, a few miles ahead." She replied, "You're supposed to be *over* it now. Do you know what you're doing, George?"

A few moments earlier, she wouldn't open her eyes—now she was telling me how to navigate. Mom flew with me frequently after that, and clearly enjoyed the adventure each time.

How long did she have to go? As it turned out, she had 20 more years. She died at 91. The Very Reverend Monsignor Laurence Higgins—the former Father Larry, who had goaded her into her first flight—flew from Tampa to Washington, D.C. to bless her on her final departure.

What did she leave me? Well, last year, at the age of 65, I got married for the first time.

I'm retired now, but I haven't bought a rocking chair.

I'm thinking of taking up aerobatics, and starting a new career.

After all—how long have I got to go?

George E. Burns

The Two Roses

*The way to love anything is to
realize that it may be lost.*

—G.K. Chesterton

What a dynamo she was! Father described her as "four-feet-eleven with an eleven-foot-four mouth." And Rosie's mouth never ceased barking out orders to the three of us—Dad, my sister and me.

"Dress warm." "Take an umbrella." "Put on your boots." "Take your vitamins." My mother was never wrong, and always ready to take on the challenge if someone disagreed with her.

A bookkeeper for many years, she had a keen interest in all kinds of topics. She had no problem defending her theories on child-rearing, nutrition, investment strategies or anything else on which she had formed an opinion. On the contrary, Rosie enjoyed a good fight. I admired the way she armed herself for battle by reading articles and books on every subject that interested her. Though it annoyed me, being argumentative was just my mother's way of showing off her new-found knowledge.

That was Rose Number One.

The new Rose—Rose Number Two—looks remarkably like her namesake. Short in stature, she has the same blue-gray eyes, engaging smile and strong voice. But there the resemblance ends.

This new Rose is quiet and agreeable. She does not argue. She never forces her opinions on anyone. In fact, one wonders if she has any. This new Rose is not an avid reader. She does not do battle with talk-show hosts and their guests while sitting in front of the TV. She does not make me angry or impatient with what I once considered intellectual arrogance. On the contrary: my dear mother has lost her intellectual capacity to Alzheimer's disease.

Now she sits alone, a vacuous look in her eyes, and my heart breaks for her. I wish she were here with me, fully engaged as she used to be, to argue and, at times, enrage.

I often think how ironic it is that the one thing I wanted to change about my mother is what I now miss the most. It would be so good to have my mother badger me, nag me, bark out her orders at me once again. "You have to take the good with the bad." That was another one of my mother's admonitions. At the time, it was just another order from Rosie. Now I find new meanings in the words. Even though she can no longer argue with me, my mother is still imparting her knowledge. She is showing me that to truly love someone means loving even their imperfections: taking the good with the bad. Rosie was right again. And by whatever name, this Rose—once so hardy and now so fragile—will remain my mother.

Jill Kimmel

Mama's Dark World

*There is no slave out of heaven like
a loving woman; and of all loving women,
there is no such slave as a mother.*

—Henry Ward Beecher

It's 10 o'clock; time to wake up Mama. Frustration washes over me because I'm sitting on my bed, covered with books. One by one, I push them aside.

I open my bedroom door into a wall of darkness. I look back into my lighted room with regret. I turn around and creep into the living room. All the lights are off and the shades are drawn. My sister Sally must have gone to bed, and I don't know where my sister Chandra is, or when she'll be home.

On the couch, covered with blankets because Mama is always cold, she lays. Her hair is standing on all ends, as it has a tendency to do, and her face is a perfect mask of peace. I give her shoulder a shake, telling her that it's 10 o'clock. Instantly, her eyes pop open and she starts to get up.

I turn to leave and go back to my bright room when she asks me to make her a cup of coffee. I swivel around and a spark of anger flicks through my eyes. The guilt quickly replaces it. How can I be angry? Every day she gets up and goes to work on barely four or five, sometimes only two, hours of sleep. She works overtime every chance she gets. I tell her not to push

76

herself, but she says we need the money. And all she's asking me for is a cup of coffee.

So I go to the kitchen. I leave the lights off, as if light would be an intrusion on Mama's dark world. I pour a cup of coffee, and add milk and sugar just the way Mama likes it. Then, I put a cup in the microwave oven we got Mama for Christmas last year. When it's done, I take it back to her. She's already dressed and sitting up on the couch.

I hand her a cup of coffee and she thanks me. I tell her Dad called and said he wasn't coming to do the work on the porch on Saturday. She simply nods her head as she drinks her coffee. Then she walks into the kitchen, placing her empty cup by the sink, reminding herself that she has to do the dishes.

All too quickly, she has to leave. I follow her to the door. She hands me my $3.60 for school the next day and kisses me on the cheek. As always, she tells me she loves me. Then she walks out the door and drives off to her job.

I watch from the door in wonder. How does she do it? How does she work all night and do errands all day? How does she raise my sisters and me on her own? She never gives up or says, "I can't go today." She never, ever doesn't get up, no matter how little sleep she's had.

I shut and lock the door. I walk silently through Mama's dark world and go back to my bright room. Before I begin again, I turn my eyes toward God and silently thank the Lord for Mama.

Amelia Chamberlain

A Mother's Advice: Be Outrageous

The essence of courage is not that your heart should not quake, but that nobody else knows that it does.

—B.B. Benson

In later years, my mother grew subdued and worn. But the woman I choose to remember is the one who was vivacious, headstrong, resourceful and full of creative energy. She could disassemble our vacuum cleaner and repair it, as well as turn our home into a Christmas wonderland every December. In leaner times, she made a formal gown out of bed sheets to wear to the Emerald Society Ball at the Waldorf Astoria Hotel, and there is no doubt in my mind that she was the most radiant woman at the affair. She always seemed strong, and I never doubted her intense love for me, even when she was angry about unaccomplished chores. We didn't often cross her; she was that kind of a woman.

Her greatest gift to me came when I was almost 13 years old and in the eighth grade. I was a good-natured kid who was significantly overweight and about to enter her first life crisis. My slim friends were deserting me for new friendships, clothes and Friday night boy-girl parties.

Popularity suddenly became a word not associated with me.

To make matters worse, the most popular girls began to make cruel remarks about me. Where I had once been accepted as a friend, my weight now made me a total outcast, and all at once I found myself rejected by even those other girls who were also "on the fringe." I was subjected to taunts, threats, cruel gestures and complete isolation. Everyone was afraid of these "popular" girls who were, in reality, tough, coarse—and older because they had been left back a grade.

My mother, realizing my plight, kept me home from school one day. She spent the whole day with me doing fun things—visiting my aunt, shopping and, of course, talking about my problem. "Don't *ever* let anyone think they're better than you," she said passionately.

Instead, she said, I should do the unexpected and outrageous, and my insecurities would disappear. Rather than cower at the lunch table, where no one wanted to sit next to me, I should announce, while looking at my watch, that there would now be an established time for people to say nasty things about me—say, in the next five minutes. I tried it. Pretending to be unaffected by the snickering and snide remarks that followed, I looked them right in the eye at the lunch table, as Mother told me to. Their reaction was total astonishment.

Somehow, I managed to work up the courage to do this little trick every day for a week. The more I did it, the more confidence I gained, and I actually began to enjoy myself as I watched the shocked look on the faces of those catty girls. I kept remembering what my mother told me. "Don't worry if people are whispering about you. It means you're interesting to them in some way. You worry when people ignore you."

By performing this charade plus other techniques my mother taught me, I was able to develop a strong sense of self-esteem that has never left me. She provided me with the courage to stand up for myself—to realize that those who needed to hurt others were the ones with the deficiencies.

I'm forever grateful for her support during those awful times. The lessons in "being outrageous" set me on a course toward a happy adolescence and have stayed with me throughout my life.

When I was in college, I came across a quote from André Gide that I've never forgotten because it perfectly summed up Mother's teachings: *It is better to be hated for what you are than loved for what you are not.*

Angela O'Loughlin Calabrese

Now, It Is a Leaf

*Imagination is more important
than knowledge.*

—Albert Einstein

We scurried around Mother like little mice when we heard her say, "Come on, *bairns,* it's time to move the furniture."

Squeals of joy would resound as we moved the sofa. "Oh, Mum, here's a sixpence . . . and over here's a threepenny piece . . . that's nine pence already."

"Alright, now let's move the big chairs."

More laughter as another child would find some pennies and another threepenny bit.

Where did the money come from? Well, in our small flat in Ferryden, a fishing village on the east coast of Scotland, our gaslight was controlled by a meter that was fed by pennies and other coins. Once every two months or so, the gas man would come to empty the meter. Mother would be given a rebate in coins, which she immediately threw under the furniture, where they would stay until she was "flat broke."

After the furniture was moved and put back in place, we'd count the retrieved coins, and Mother would say to our oldest sister, Nan, and our brother George, "First things first. Now go down to the bakery for six French cakes and we'll celebrate at teatime. Then we'll decide what we'll do with the rest of the cash."

We licked our lips and our fingers as we ate the small cupcakes covered with icing, each one a different color. We five children were given one cake apiece, leaving one for Mother.

We learned from our mother, a widow bringing up her children alone on a small military pension and whatever she could scrape together by sewing for people, that you always make the best of everything that happens, and try to have fun doing it.

In Ferryden in the bleak winter time, the daylight faded out early and crept into darkness by 4:00 P.M. We did our homework and ate supper, usually a hearty soup, or boiled potatoes slathered with real butter. For dessert, Mother would cut into a Java orange as big as a grapefruit and divide it among us. Mother knew nothing about Vitamin C, but she was sure that the oranges kept us from getting colds. Sometimes, bread pudding or apple dumplings would fill us up.

Then we would all gather around the kitchen table with pieces of paper and a paint box, which held eight colors and one brush. Mother taught us how to draw flowers and paint them, passing the brush and paints around. I recall one evening when my little sister looked somewhat unhappy. "What's the matter, my bonnie lass?" asked Mother.

"One of my flower petals looks like a leaf," my sister replied, close to tears because her flower petal didn't look like a flower petal.

"Let me see," said Mother. "Oh, yes. Well, paint it green. Now, it is a leaf."

Margo Marshall-Olmstead

READER/CUSTOMER CARE SURVEY

If you are enjoying this book, please help us serve you better and meet your changing needs by taking a few minutes to complete this survey. Please fold it & drop it in the mail. **As a thank you, we will send you a gift.**

Name: _____

Address: _____

_____

Tel. # _____

(1) Gender: 1) ____ Female 2) ____ Male

(2) Age: 1)____ 18-25 4)____ 46-55
2)____ 26-35 5)____ 56-65
3)____ 36-45 6)____ 65+

(3) Marital status:

1)____ Married 3)____ Single 5)____ Widowed
2)____ Divorced 4)____ Partner

(4) Is this book: 1)____ Purchased for self?
2)____ Purchased for others?
3)____ Received as gift?

(5) How did you find out about this book?

1)____ Catalog 2)____ Store Display
Newspaper
3)____ Best Seller List
4)____ Article/Book Review
5)____ Advertisement
Magazine
6)____ Feature Article
7)____ Book Review
8)____ Advertisement
9)____ Word of Mouth
A)____ T.V./Talk Show (Specify) _____
B)____ Radio/Talk Show (Specify) _____
C)____ Professional Referral _____
D)____ Other (Specify) _____

(6) What subject areas do you enjoy reading most? (Rank in order of enjoyment)

1)____ Women's Issues/ 5)____ New Age/
Relationships Altern. Healing
2)____ Business Self Help 6)____ Aging
3)____ Soul/Spirituality/ 7)____ Parenting
Inspiration 8)____ Diet/Nutrition/
4)____ Recovery Exercise/Health

(14) What do you look for when choosing a personal growth book?
(Rank in order of importance)

1)____ Subject 3)____ Author
2)____ Title 4)____ Price
Cover Design 5)____ In Store Location

(19) When do you buy books?
(Rank in order of importance)

1)____ Christmas
2)____ Valentine's Day
3)____ Birthday
4)____ Mother's Day
5)____ Other (Specify _____

(23) Where do you buy your books?
(Rank in order of frequency of purchases)

1)____ Bookstore 6)____ Gift Store
2)____ Price Club 7)____ Book Club
3)____ Department Store 8)____ Mail Order
4)____ Supermarket/ 9)____ T.V. Shopping
Drug Store A)____ Airport
5)____ Health Food Store

Which book are you currently reading? _____

Additional comments you would like to make to help us serve you better.

_____

_____

Thank You !!

NO POSTAGE
NECESSARY
IF MAILED
IN THE
UNITED STATES

BUSINESS REPLY MAIL

FIRST CLASS MAIL PERMIT NO 45 DEERFIELD BEACH, FL

POSTAGE WILL BE PAID BY ADDRESSEE

HEALTH COMMUNICATIONS
3201 SW 15TH STREET
DEERFIELD BEACH, FL 33442-9875

The Last Lesson

Love is never lost. If not reciprocated, it will flow back and soften and purify the heart.

—Washington Irving

I had just left my office one Tuesday night in April 1981 when I was gripped by a feeling that I should visit my mother. She was in a hospital because of heart disease and kidney failure. She was recovering and had been there for a few weeks, but something told me that I should visit her that night. I had just finished a full day of seeing patients and was exhausted, but I did not question this feeling.

Upon my arrival at the hospital I went to her room, but she was not there. Nobody had informed me of this change and I began to get anxious. I eventually located her in intensive care, waiting to be dialyzed. I looked at her and immediately knew that this was the end, that her life of 72 years was going to culminate within a few moments. But first she was going to teach me about death.

I had not been there five years earlier, when my father passed away. But I had visited him often as he deteriorated from the brain tumor. His death was something we could prepare for. I arrived at the hospital about five minutes after he died to say my final good-bye to him. While his illness had drawn us together, my father and I had never been very close. My mother, however, was a different story.

83

I grew up an anxious and overprotected youngster and spent a great deal of my adolescence alternating between pleasing Mom and rebelling against her. I spent a lot of time with her, looking for messages of unconditional love and acceptance.

I never found them. Rather, I found mixed messages of love but also, "You could do better." My mother always tried to teach me what she thought was right, but this was based on her limited experiences, her upbringing, and the superstitious thinking of the time within the Jewish culture. She always had a lesson to teach me, and her comments made me feel as if I was not good enough. I wanted her love and acceptance without her comments.

However, that night in April, she had one more lesson to teach me.

I found her in a bed having difficulty breathing. I asked her how she was and she said, "You know the doctor—ask him." At that point, her breathing became more labored and she started to turn deathly pale. I went over and took her in my arms to hold her. She looked at me and, with her last breath, said that she loved me. And then she died.

They tried to resuscitate her, but I knew that it was futile. And I also knew that somehow she had waited for me to come to her before she would take that final breath. It seemed ironic but also so fitting that she had chosen me to be with her, after I'd spent a lifetime seeking reassurance that she loved me.

And so my mother's final lesson to me was to show me that in her own way and for her time, her love for me had always been there, and she had always been fully accepting of me. Her wanting me to do better was my mother's way of wanting her son to have more. If not unconditional, her love was certainly unselfish.

And in a final act of unselfish devotion, she waited for me before she died. I am forever grateful to my mother for what she taught me about love.

Joel Kimmel

Leaving Home

*One of the oldest human needs is
having someone to wonder where you are
when you don't come home at night.*

—Margaret Mead

As many young people have done before her, Molly left her home in small-town America and moved to New York City to seek her fame and fortune. Molly's was from Columbia, South Carolina, and her dream was to be a copywriter in a big advertising agency on Madison Avenue. Armed with a liberal arts degree from the University of South Carolina, blessed with a vivacious personality, blonde hair and wholesome good looks, she said good-bye to her mom in the summer of 1970 and headed north.

When Molly was eight years old, her father died of a heart attack in the middle of a Fourth of July barbecue right in their backyard. Molly's mother never remarried, despite many overtures. She and Molly's father were a fabled couple who had been inseparable and very much in love. After he died, her mother told Molly she would never remarry because that had been her perfect love, and nothing would ever compare. Molly never saw her mother despondent. Like her daughter, she had a warm and engaging personality. She devoted herself to helping others in the community, reading to the blind and fund-raising for the children's hospital.

Of course, she was sad when Molly announced that she would be leaving Columbia. She would miss her, and she was worried about all that urban blight in New York. The other reason she was distressed about Molly leaving was Bob, Molly's childhood sweetheart. It had never entered her mind that Molly and Bob would not get married after college, settle nearby, and raise a family. Even when Molly began to show signs of restlessness in her junior year at USC, she thought it would pass and that whatever her ambitions were, she could fulfill them right there. But that didn't happen. Instead, Molly told Bob she loved him but had to "get it out of her system." She implored him to understand that she was not ready to settle down, that something was driving her to experience other things, and she hoped he would wait for her.

This was very unreasonable, Molly's mother pointed out. As loving and understanding as Bob was, she didn't think Molly had the right to ask that of him. "You will lose him, Molly," she warned. "And you will find that there is nothing more important than the love of a good man. You can visit all the great cities of the world, make lots of money and have a brilliant career, but all of that won't make you happy. What counts, Molly, is to have someone waiting there when you turn the key in the door and get home at night."

Molly thought her mother was projecting her own feelings of sadness and loneliness. Besides, she didn't intend to be without Bob, whom she had persuaded to give her just one year. During that year, she argued passionately, she would be home for holidays and vacations; he could visit her and they'd do the town together. She would call daily, she promised, and tell him of her wonderful adventures while she was being trained as a copywriter at a big, famous agency. And then she would return to Columbia. A strapping, handsome fellow who adored Molly and knew it would be a mistake to hold her against her will, Bob reluctantly agreed. They had a pact. He would join his father's real estate development firm in downtown Columbia, and they would be "unofficially" engaged for the year Molly was in New York.

The first three months of her new life in New York, Molly thought she was in a dream. She had landed a job at a prestigious agency where she was assigned to a big account—even though all she did was write copy for coupons that offered "Buy one, get one free." She did talk to Bob every day, or almost every day.

In the months that followed Molly was generally not at home until close to 10 o'clock at night, and when she called home, she sounded hurried all the time. "You're working too hard," her mother told her. "Slow down. What are you trying to prove?" Molly didn't know what she was trying to prove, but she did know her job was expanding, there were always deadlines, there was more copy to write . . . plus the promise of a promotion soon. So she worked late, worked weekends and began to miss some of Bob's calls. Sometimes she was too tired to return his calls. When they would talk, several days later, he would plaintively ask her if she still loved him.

Molly didn't know. But when almost a year had passed, and she was given the opportunity to either go to the Virgin Islands to shoot a commercial or spend her vacation time in Columbia, she made the choice that proved decisive. From that point on, there was no stopping her. She rose to vice president in five years. Before she was 30, she was named senior vice president and creative director on a major soft-drink account. She had her own two-bedroom apartment on East End Avenue, with a terrace and a view of the river. She wore designer clothes and had her hair done twice a week at the best salon on East 57th Street. She never stopped to think if she was happy. She was too busy to wonder how she felt about anything.

Bob stopped calling after she missed that trip, and Molly heard from her mother soon after that he was engaged to the daughter of a wealthy banker. Shortly after that, her mother sent her an article from *The State,* the leading newspaper in Columbia, with photos of Bob and his bride on their wedding day. It was a grand wedding at the antebellum home of the bride's parents in Charleston. The lawn was covered with pink and white striped tents, and the bride had a contingent of eight bridesmaids. She was very beautiful, Molly thought, and lucky to have married such a steady, level-headed guy.

Molly was truly happy for Bob. She was sorry they had just

drifted apart, but so much in life was timing, she told herself. And, at the time, she really was not ready to be his wife, settle in the South, and ignore all the adventures she knew were ahead.

Then one day, a curious thing happened. Molly was at the airport in Los Angeles, waiting for the red-eye back to New York, when a terrible sadness overcame her. Without warning, her eyes filled with tears. Sensing that she was losing control of her emotions, she hastily boarded the plane. In the dimly-lit first-class compartment, she put her seat back and closed her eyes, determined to figure out what was bothering her.

A cheerful and optimistic person by nature, she was baffled by this depression that wouldn't lift. It was as though a black curtain had descended over her, and despite all the bright spots in her life at the moment, she could see only darkness. If anything, she should have been exhilarated, having just sold a campaign to one of the agency's toughest clients. And among the many messages on her answering machine, there was one from a real estate broker in Connecticut, telling her that her offer on an old farmhouse with five acres had been accepted. For some time, she had felt the need to have a weekend place out of the city, where she could have a garden and be awakened by birds instead of garbage trucks or police sirens. Surely, that was cause for celebration.

She turned her face to the window, and staring out at the vast darkness, she suddenly remembered her mother's words, so many years ago, about putting the key in the door and finding someone when you get home.

That was it! Her apartment was absolutely lovely, with Art Deco furniture and antique rugs throughout. The Connecticut house would be warm and inviting, down to the last detail. But there was no one waiting for her—anywhere. Her mother's words came back to her now, with incredible clarity. "You can be in one little town all your life, Molly, and still experience everything important in the universe, if you're with the man you love. Love is the biggest adventure there is."

Ten years later, Molly was visiting her mother in Columbia at Christmas. She was in the local Wal-Mart buying an extra string of lights for the tree when she heard someone call her name. He was tall, with dark wavy hair streaked with gray. He had put on a little weight, but Bob was as handsome as ever.

It had been almost 20 years since they had seen each other, but she felt as though nothing had changed. They had a cup of hot chocolate together, and Bob told her he was divorced and visiting his parents in Columbia for the holidays. He took her hand as they walked to her car under a luminous, starry sky.

Within three months, Molly had resigned, put her apartment up for sale, and moved in with Bob. Soon after, they were married. From that day on, my cousin Molly knew that whenever she put that key in the door, someone would be waiting for her when she got home.

Betty Sue Hardin

The Parrot

Eager to buy a special gift for his aged mother, the doting son came across a highly articulate parrot and decided it was the kind of exotic gift she would enjoy. He had it delivered.

Several weeks later, he visited his mother. "Tell me," he said, "did you receive the beautiful parrot I sent you?"

"I did indeed. You are a thoughtful son."

"Were you pleased, Mother?"

"Absolutely. It seemed to me at first that he would be small and stringy, but the soup was delicious."

The son leaped from his seat. "You *ate* it? But that bird could speak seven languages!"

His mother, equally startled, said, "Well, in that case, why didn't he say something when I put him in the pot?"

Anonymous

Mom, the Original Recycler

*Common sense is genius dressed
in its working clothes.*

—Ralph Waldo Emerson

Each Thursday night, my neighbors and I carefully place our three recycling containers on the curb. One container has newspapers and cardboard, stacked and tied. One has cans, rinsed and crushed. The third has glass bottles and plastic containers. We all feel so good that we're doing our bit to save the environment.

The environment? Landfills? Biodegradable materials? Mom didn't know these terms when she was raising a family; her recycling was a result of common sense and necessity.

I remember so many things Mom used to do to save a few pennies here and there. However, her motivation was more than economics; it was an integral part of her belief that wasting anything is a sin. As a result, nothing was ever thrown away without first considering all possible uses for it. If you think we recycle today, you should have been around Mom when . . .

Paper bags were carefully cut up and folded into neat book covers to protect our schoolbooks.

Lids from soup cans were hammered into markers for our street games of "potsy" and hopscotch.

Old sheets and pillowcases were transformed into ironing board covers.

Old shirts and pajamas became cleaning rags—but not before removing the buttons, which accumulated in the sewing box.

String and rubber bands were saved in the "junk drawer."

An empty mayonnaise jar held laundry detergent, to avoid carrying the big box to the laundromat each wash day and, in the process, perhaps spilling and wasting some.

If shopping bags had had a five-cent redemption value in those days, Mom would be a very wealthy woman because they were hoarded and saved like gold!

Mom's recycling habits have certainly been passed on to me. I still have a garage filled with brown paper bags, which I use for mailing packages. I, too, have a quantity of rubber bands that I can't bear to part with. I have a box of buttons that I keep adding to each time I buy something with extra buttons. How can I possibly sort these out and throw any away? It would be a sin, and besides, who knows when I'll need that extra rhinestone or red plastic button? . . .

My "junk drawer" overflows with safety pins, paper clips, snips of ribbon and scraps of wrapping paper. I'll never be able to throw away any of these things, I know, because Mom taught me it's a sin to waste anything.

It's a lesson that the rest of the world seems just beginning to appreciate and understand. But not for Mom. Fifty years ago, my mother was already preserving the environment and saving the Earth.

Patricia L. Aho

The Strangers

*If we were to wake up some morning and
find that everyone was the same race, creed and
color, we would find some other causes
for prejudice by noon.*

—Senator George Aiken

They first began coming in 1940, just after the war began. It was for me, at the time an eight-year-old, the first glimpse of a universe beyond the treasured confines of my childhood and my safe family world in Brooklyn.

At first it was just children, then later whole family units: the human detritus of a world gone war mad. They came from Poland and Germany and France, brought by relief agencies, usually housed with relatives and friends.

My first experience with them was in the fall of 1941 when America, still at peace, viewed from afar the rising storm that would soon envelop us all. The first day of school that September brought Aaron W. to our class. His younger sister, Sara, was in the grade below.

They were the Jews: the Jews from Germany, who could not speak English except for a few halting words learned in their flight from their home to Denmark, then to England, then to our streets and our school.

They were Jews, refugees in an ethnic enclave that knew only descendants from Ireland and England and Scandinavia.

They were sad-eyed, frightened children from another place, foreign and threatening, who had seen a life that we, the progeny of the American experience, had been spared. They dressed in clothes that didn't fit, and their decidedly foreign-looking shoes (look at those shoes) were the focus of many a derisive joke among our class of 10-year-olds.

I told my mother of these interlopers, these strangers, so foreign and so unlike real people.

She would say that they came from hardships and experiences we could never imagine, and that she hoped that her son would treat them with respect. "Try to be friends," she implored. "They are alone here in a new country. Think how you would feel in a place where you didn't even know the language."

Through the fall and the winter, Aaron and Sara began to meld into the commonality of school days. Remarkably, they began to function with increasing skill in our classes, in which only English was spoken and where no concession was ever made to their lack of knowledge of our language.

Aaron, with his small frame, even withstood the physical taunts of older boys and kept a quiet dignity born of some inner resource of strength. In the unreasoned nomenclature of pre-adolescents, he was no longer even "Aaron." He became "Harry."

My mother would always counsel me, "Be open to the ways of others. You can learn much about life from other people. Learning comes from allowing you to experience not only your life and ways, but from observing and being with people different from you."

Still, a fear of disapproval kept me from choosing Aaron as my friend. After all, he was the stranger. He was the Jew kid from Germany.

In the spring, Aaron's mother and father came, uniting the family for the first time in two years. Then a strange thing happened. Aaron came to me and asked if I would like to be with him and his family at the Passover Seder—the first they would celebrate together in America.

I was confused. Why me? I didn't know what it all meant, this strange, foreign religious ritual. I said no.

I related this unsought invitation to my mother. In her grand, sweet, knowing way, she said simply, "You should be honored to be asked. It is a part of Jewish tradition, a tradition that goes back through centuries. It was an invitation that came out of friendship and caring."

I attended the Seder that year at the family table of Aaron and Sara. Only after more maturing graced my understanding did I realize what it meant to me.

"Harry" and I became friends, real friends, in the ensuing years. We graduated from grammar school together and went on to high school. Then in the warp and woof of life's fabric, the comings and goings of time, we moved away from each other to different cities and places and experiences. Contacts and letters became less frequent, then they ceased.

In her 55th year, my mother was stricken with heart disease, the legacy of a rheumatic heart condition she suffered as a young girl. She had a coronary bypass operation in a hospital in Houston—a procedure that at that time was new.

The evening after the operation, as my father and I held vigil and talked about the success of the procedure we were visited by one of the cardiologists who assisted with the operation.

He was Dr. Aaron W.

Yustin Wallrapp

A Message from Heaven

A mother is not a person to lean on but a person to make leaning unnecessary.

—Dorothy Canfield Fisher

Four months after my mother died, she sent me a message that made it possible for me to face the future without her and come to terms with my grief. She was beautiful, feisty and the most willful creature I'd ever met. My father lovingly called her "Mighty Mouth" because she had such strong opinions. She was constantly writing letters to editors, phoning her representatives in Congress, and standing up at school board or other community meetings to voice her opinions and take a stand for the underdog. A lifelong liberal Democrat, she was an ardent supporter of many social causes. Even when I disagreed with her and called her a "bleeding-heart liberal," I admired and loved her for the passion and commitment she felt for those less fortunate. She was on everyone's mailing list, and even when we were strapped for money and bills were unpaid, she would somehow find $10 or $20 to donate to handicapped veterans, animal welfare, cancer research, unwed mothers—you name it.

I was a timid, dependent child who totally lacked the confidence my mother seemed to possess naturally. From grade school through college, I was in a constant state of anxiety and self-doubt. I was certain I'd fail my exams. My mother was always there to buoy me and urge me to believe I could pass. Even when

97

I did, I never felt secure. Throughout my life, I was convinced I could not take on any challenges unless my mother was there to support and encourage me.

When Mother was diagnosed with ovarian cancer, my world came apart. Not only because of the pain and suffering I knew she would have to go through, but because of the terrible feelings of dread I experienced, even at 42 years of age, about not being able to function without her. I am ashamed to say that I was full of thoughts about how I would manage without her when I should have been thinking of her and the disease that ravaged her so quickly. Instead, I worried that she would die before I took my law boards and if she did how could I possibly pass?

My mother knew I felt helpless and frightened, like a small child. Even at the end, with morphine doses increasing to the point where she was barely conscious most of the time, she would take my hand and pat it, as though I were the one who needed comforting.

One day, when we all knew the end was near, I broke down and told her what was in my heart, even though I'd tried so hard to be as brave as she was.

"Don't leave me, Mother," I cried, holding her emaciated frame. "I need to know you're with me," I sobbed. "Please, Mother, stay with me always."

She slipped back on the pillows and looked at me with some of the old fire in her eyes.

"You want me to do *what?*" she inquired. "You silly girl. How many times have I told you you'll be fine." Then, in a barely audible voice, she said, "Besides, you'll hear from me now and then." She turned her face from me and drifted off then, but I was sure I saw an impish grin light her features, just like she used to look when she was in a playful mood. Those were the last words she said to me.

All she ever had to do with me was get a little terse or gently prod me, and I'd "grow up" fast. But four months after her death, I was in a state of near collapse. I had to take my law boards and was paralyzed with fear. The morning of the exam, I prayed to my mother to help me get out of bed. No response. Then I prayed to her to help me get dressed. Silence. I kept on praying until I was on the F train headed to Brooklyn, where the exam was being given. Despite my trembling hands and racing heart, she didn't answer me.

Through the grueling exam, I kept calling upon my mother while trying to concentrate on complex legal arguments that hurt my brain. After years of building a career in a totally unrelated field, I had decided to get a law degree, and now that the six years of study crammed into a full-time job were coming to an end, I was convinced I couldn't do it. Mother wasn't there, so how could I?

The remarkable thing is that my mother did finally answer my prayers, in her own inimitable way. It was early evening, and the lights of Manhattan glowed softly across the Hudson River from my apartment in Fort Lee. After an exhausting day taking the exam, I'd stopped trying to summon my mother. I was watching the evening news when I heard some noises in the bedroom, as though something had fallen to the floor. My puppy, Dakota, was sitting quietly at my feet, so I knew it wasn't due to his usual pranks trying to wrestle with my pantyhose.

I put on the light and looked around the bedroom. There on the carpet in front of the bookcase was an envelope with photos of my mother as a young woman, a packet of her letters sent to me when I was away at college, and a carved ivory jewelry box containing her prized collection of antique jewelry. They were among the precious things I wanted to find just the right place for, but hadn't had the heart to make any decisions about.

The fact that they had fallen from the top of the bookcase was certainly surprising, since they were all securely in place on a wide shelf. But what was really strange to me was the way they had fallen and were grouped together, like an artful photograph, letters on one side, photos on the other, and the elegant jewelry box in the middle. It was as though they had been arranged that way.

I know my mother was speaking to me that evening, and what she was saying was that she knew I could do it without her. I could, and I did.

Paula Kaufman, Attorney-at-Law

Witticism

A great many witticisms have been attributed to Dorothy Parker. Here's one about mothers that you may not have heard:

Trapped by an insufferable bore at a social gathering, Ms. Parker was being tortured with long, tedious stories about how wonderful and charming people found him to be.

Finally, he said with great self-righteousness, "What it amounts to is that I simply can't bear fools."

To which Dorothy Parker replied, "Odd. Your mother apparently could."

The Dancing Broom

*The clearest sign of wisdom is
continued cheerfulness.*

—Montaigne

My mother had all the wonderful attributes that Hallmark
could ever wish for as reasons to honor mothers on their day. I
want to share with you her gift for enjoying life.

Mother's life was not an easy one. She brought up three children during the Depression. Dad lost his business and had to
depend upon finding daily work in an ever-frustrating attempt
to support his family. But Mother's marvelous gift of turning
things around helped immeasurably, with the result that we
never thought of ourselves as poor. She always saw the glass
half full and not half empty, and many things she did reflected
that attitude.

When potatoes were all that was available for dinner, mother
had at least 66 ways to prepare them. My favorites were potato
pancakes with applesauce and potato soup. Chicken salad was a
real treat when we could afford it, made from a chicken that had
already provided two or three meals.

When Dad was expected home after looking for work all day,
Mother had us look for him out the window. If he lifted his fingers in a victory sign, we knew we would have steak for dinner—
and french fried potatoes! We had fun, and Mother was the

instigator of these good times—even in bad times.

Weekends were spent at the zoo. Our special friend was the monkey born on my older brother's birthday. We were all certain he recognized us when we came to visit him. Other times, we played games in the park with the folks. Remember, we didn't know we were poor.

The best memory I have of my mother is her dancing. She and my dad were good dancers, but unless there was a family gathering, there was no opportunity or money to go dancing. But that didn't hinder my mother. When she cleaned the house, her radio always played the popular tunes of the day, and she would dance, clutching the broom handle like a partner. Away she flew, across the room, in perfect rhythm. What a sight to behold! What joy and contentment she exuded!

I was blessed with a mother who taught me that life is often what you make it. We may have been poor, but that didn't stop us from thinking that we had a wealth of tremendous advantages.

Ethel Reiner Gorelick

The Thin Red Line

A truth spoken before its time is dangerous.

—Greek proverb

Before I was born, my parents had two children, a boy named Charley and a girl named Sonny. It was a happy family until Charley died. He was only 15.

According to my mother, that's precisely why I came into the picture. My mother had a strong belief that no child should be an only child, so despite the fact that she was in her mid-40s, she got pregnant again. At that time, such a late pregnancy was considered dangerous, and her doctor was seriously concerned that she wouldn't carry me to the full term and have a normal birth. As you can tell from this story, I made it.

Growing up in the shadow of Charley's memory was not easy. My mother got rid of most every reminder of Charley but one photo, a drawer full of report cards, and his Boy Scout badges. Competing with Charley's report cards (he was smarter) was tough. After all, I couldn't beat the heck out of him. In fact, the mere mention of his name sent my mother into tears and my father into a deep depression. We rarely brought up the subject.

This is what happened to Charley: Sonny came home from school one day and asked Charley what he wanted for dinner because my parents were out, and Sonny was in charge of fixing dinner. Charley said steak. My mother phoned to see if everything was alright, and

103

Sonny said everything was fine and she was going to cook steak for dinner. Then Charley went up to his room and died.

Sonny found the body and had to stay alone with Charley until my parents returned home. After an experience like that, it was understandable that she never wanted to talk about it. No one wanted to talk about it.

When I reached the appropriate age, my mother told me Charley had died of a respiratory infection because there were no antibiotics at the time he was sick. I bought the story hook, line and sinker—until I visited a psychic years later.

Like most people—and especially cynical New Yorkers—I was skeptical about the powers of a psychic. At the time, it was something I didn't take too seriously; but on an impulse, I went for a reading. To give him as little help as possible, I said nothing about myself. I just sat opposite him and defiantly said, "Go on."

He did. Alex told me that two spirits were with me at all times. One was a man with white hair who wore a 10-gallon hat and had a "terrible smell" about him. That description fit my dead father to a tee. Even though he had never been in Texas and always looked like a dapper Manhattan businessman, that was his favorite hat. As for the "terrible smell," my father practically chain-smoked Garcia Vega Regalia cigars, and he did have an aura about him.

The other spirit, Alex said, was a teenage boy, around 15. Alex saw a thin red line through his heart.

I was flabbergasted. Nobody had ever told me anything about Charley's heart. Alex asked me what was wrong, since I obviously looked stunned. I didn't tell him that I thought he was mistaken, since this was news to me. All I said was, "Are you sure?"

Again, he went into a trance and slowly repeated to me that he saw a thin red line down the center of my brother's heart. It was unmistakable, he said.

My mother was ahead of her time in many ways, so she was open to experiences with the occult. I called her as soon as I got home from the reading. When I told her about my father, she was really impressed. How on earth could anyone guess about the 10-gallon hat, she wondered. After all, it was not common attire in New York City.

"But he got Charley all wrong," I said. "He said he died of a heart condition."

There was complete silence on the other end of the phone. When she regained her composure, my mother told me the truth.

Charley had been born with a congenital heart condition. The opening between the chambers of his heart had a small hole. That was fine until he reached puberty, when the heart or opening somehow was supposed to close, but it didn't. Charley then became very ill and spent most of his double-digit years in a wheelchair. There was nothing the medical profession could do about it. There was no open-heart surgery at the time.

"I didn't tell you," my mother sighed, "because I was afraid that you'd be afraid to have a child."

I had already had a son by the time I visited the psychic, so having my own children was not an issue anymore. Evan, my son, has no congenital heart condition. Neither do my sister's two children.

Even now I struggle with the way my mother kept the truth from me. The child in me often feels betrayed, even angry, for being led to believe the lie about Charley. But the parent in me understands that immutable, instinctive urge to shield your child from any possible pain. My mother did not think she was deceiving me; she felt she was protecting me. It is, I believe, one of the most difficult challenges that we face: how to be completely truthful and a mother at the same time. Like walking a thin red line, we must look into our hearts for guidance.

Carol Moser

My Mother's Cookbook

*And the best bread was of my mother's
making—the best in all the land!*

—Sir Henry James

My husband and I were living and working abroad when
news came that Mother had died. I took the first flight I could back
to her small town in Oklahoma, feeling guilty and sad—although
we'd always been close, circumstances had kept us apart in recent
years.

Mother had always lived very simply, and at the time of her
death she rented three small rooms just a few blocks from where
she was born. She left my brother and me nothing; the fact is, she
had nothing to leave. But on the day that my brother, my aunt and
I cleared out her apartment, discarding almost everything, I found
one item I wanted to keep.

It was her old cookbook, held together by a large rubber band
and stuffed with clippings from newspapers and magazines, most
of them yellow with age, and with recipes written on anything and
everything—index cards, note paper, old letters and greeting
cards, little scraps of paper, even old bills and shopping lists. The
back cover and spine were still intact, but the front cover was torn
loose and so faded that the words *Cook Book* were barely
discernible. Still, I couldn't resist the idea of taking it home.

As soon as I could, I set aside time to examine my treasure.

106

Carefully, I removed the rubber band and the front cover. The title page was as brown and dry as a tobacco leaf, and on it my grandmother had written, "To my daughter on her wedding day, December 5, 1932."

On the inside front cover, my mother had copied the lines, "God is more pleased by some sweet human use / Than by the learned book of the recluse." I pictured my mother, a young bride of 17, opening the book for the first time, writing the lines carefully, thinking of the meals she would cook and dreaming the dreams young girls dream.

I turned the page. Here were the detailed instructions on "How to Make This Cook Book Your Master Recipe File." The book was a three-ring binder, and the homemaker was advised to cut recipes neatly from other sources, paste them onto the provided blank sheets, and index them properly. Mother had disregarded these directions entirely and stuck recipes willy-nilly anywhere in the book. How she ever found anything in it had always been a mystery to me.

I decided to try to put this hodgepodge of material into some sort of chronological order. As I worked, I began to realize that the story of my mother's life was emerging from these odds and ends of paper. In a way, so was the history of a whole generation of women who married and raised families during the Depression, the War and the postwar years.

The oldest finding took me back as far as 1920. It was a canceled check, with a recipe for a cranberry salad on the back, written by my grandmother and passed down to my mother. Other recipes from Mother's youth, written in her familiar, yet younger, hand, revealed her teenage love for sweets—such treats as divinity fudge and marshmallow candy. Digging deeper, I found the recipe for sand tarts, the first cookies I ever baked as a child. And then there was *the* birthday cake.

It was the cake Mother had baked whenever there was something important—like a birthday—to celebrate. The cake was tall, delicious and elegant, and in her cookbook I found the recipe, "Chiffon Birthday Cake for 20 People," which had been featured in *McCall's Magazine* a few years after the war.

I have baked the same cake several times since, and each time I do, I feel a strong connection to my mother and my past, and never fail to think of all the happy moments I owe to her.

But Mother's cookbook brought back some sad memories as well. I was also reminded that, while she was making life so pleasant for me, her own life wasn't turning out the way she had hoped.

The Depression had hit with a vengeance, and Mother, like most other women in America, had to cut corners. Daddy tried to make a living as a musician but couldn't, and worked with the Civilian Conservation Corps for a while until he eventually became a policeman. It was a period of meals made from cheap cuts of meat, if there was meat at all, and from extenders: meals like ham loaf, chicken and turkey loaf, veal salad, corn-and-frankfurter main dish, and corned-beef and macaroni salad. A newspaper clipping from March 7, 1935 bore a recipe for snow ice that required nothing more than a little vanilla, sugar, egg whites and snow. On it my mother had written the single exclamation, "Yummm."

Deprivation and hard times never seemed to faze my mother, who had only modest and simple aspirations. What she wanted out of life was a pretty little house somewhere and a snug, peaceful existence with her husband and children. My father's aspirations, however, were quite different.

Turning the cookbook's pages and unearthing so many budget-conscious dishes, I wondered how well he had taken to a casserole of cabbage and tomatoes or to a luncheon suggestion of green beans, bran muffins and fruit whip. There had always been something of the dandy and connoisseur about Daddy, and it was difficult to picture him, even as a young man, smiling through too many meals that didn't at least *sound* elegant.

When I was four, the war in Europe was raging, and my father was called into active service in Hawaii. During this period, my mother, the dutiful Army officer's wife, amassed a great collection of recipes using pineapple. After Pearl Harbor was attacked, my mother, then three months pregnant, and I were evacuated and went to live with my grandmother in Oklahoma, where we waited for the war to end.

The clippings of this period evoke strong memories. How to stretch those ration stamps seemed to be the major theme of every other magazine article. And how Mother stretched. And substituted. Or simply did without. "One cup" sugar was crossed out in recipe after recipe and "one-half cup" and even "one-quarter cup" was written in. "Cream" inevitably became "milk." "Butter" became either "shortening" or the curt abbreviation "Subst." One recipe for Lemon Yolk Sponge Cake had so many substitutions written in that Mother had scratched out the name and rechristened it "Lemon Joke Sponge Cake." She hadn't lost her sense of humor.

Nor had she lost her energy. She raised chickens and planted a Victory Garden, and from this period in her life I unearthed enough salad suggestions, enough ways to prepare vegetables, enough things to do with eggs and chicken to fill a good-size cookbook.

The war ended. On the back of a recipe for twice-baked potatoes a movie ad announced, "Gable's back and Garson's got him." Clark Gable was a civilian again, and so were millions of others, including Daddy, ready to start their "real life," the good life!

The clippings from the period reflected the new prosperity. "Melt six tablespoons of *butter*," "Pork, Sweet and Tender," *"Cheese Souffle: Rich and Smooth."* The lean years were indeed over.

My father, who hated scrimping, threw himself into the postwar period with enthusiasm. He discovered aluminum foil, the electric blender, the barbecue, the freezer and suburbia. He discovered foreign food: In my search I found recipes for pizza, paella, tacos, Bavarian dressing, Greek bread and Chinese stir-fry. He also discovered the casual life and built a thing called a patio on the back of our new house in Arkansas. The rest of the country was going casual too: the words *convenient, easy* and *fast* became as essential as the main ingredient to every recipe.

My mother loved that house in Arkansas, the first and last my parents ever owned. She once confided to me that the three years we spent there were the happiest of her life.

My romantic father, however, decided to abandon his gray flannel suit and his office job at the Veterans Administration and become a gentleman farmer. ("Serve a Country Ham" my mother had cut from a magazine, and "It's an Old-Fashioned Thanksgiving") He failed miserably. So on a whim he moved us all to Costa Rica. Mother's recipe collection included no fewer than four versions of *arroz con frijoles* (rice and beans), a dish she learned to adore there. But again, my father's dreams did not come true, and we returned to the States, broke but together.

Not all the discoveries I made that day were easily categorized. Clues about the later years of my mother's life, in particular, were hard to identify. I know what I *wanted* to find, and had I assumed the role of fiction writer, I know what I would have invented. There would be recipes for intimate, candlelit dinners for two—Mother and Daddy after my brother and I grew up and made our own lives. Or perhaps there would be cozy articles on cooking for the grandchildren or suggestions for the big family-reunion dinner.

But they were not in my mother's cookbook. My father, always the dreamer, drifted out of my mother's life into some final mysterious adventure. My brother, after years in Vietnam, made the Army his career, and our work took my husband and me thousands of miles from home. We often urged Mother to come live with us, but she always refused, saying she wanted to make her own life.

I like to think that those last years in her hometown were, if not happy, at least contented ones. Certainly they were busy. From this period I found two little scraps. Neither one was a recipe, but both were connected with food.

One was an article written by a Wichita columnist who had stumbled onto the small café where my mother baked part-time. The column raved about Mother's "perfect" cinnamon rolls and her other culinary delights—doughnuts, pies and brownies. Mother was briefly a local celebrity, and I'm sure that being praised for her baking pleased her more than any other honor she could have received.

Finally, there was her last shopping list, which she must have written the morning she was taken ill so suddenly and rushed to the hospital, never to return. I had found it on top of the refrigerator the day we cleaned her apartment and had absentmindedly slipped it into the front pages of the cookbook. Like many women of her generation, Mother had respect for food. She knew what was good, and she found goodness in the simplest foods. Although Mother liked to experiment and loved exotic dishes, she was always happiest with the plainest meals. I think of all my findings I'll cherish that shopping list most. It read, "Eggs, spuds, beans, rice."

There was a pecan tree growing in the alley behind Mother's little apartment. It didn't seem to belong to anyone, so Mother, with her usual thrift, would pick up the pecans that fell to the ground and then spend evenings patiently shelling them in front of her TV. On that sad day after the funeral, my aunt and I came into the kitchen and found my brother standing in front of the open refrigerator with a jar of nutmeats in his hand and a desolate look on his usually stoical face.

We just stood there looking at that little jar until my aunt said, "Tell you what. Why don't we take those home and make a pecan pie for dinner?"

In spite of the painful event that had brought us all together again for the first time in several years, the mood became quite cheerful back in my aunt's kitchen. The pie was in the oven. The room was warm and bright. Everything smelled delicious. It was already starting to get dark on that early November day, and there was a winter chill in the air. My uncle and cousins came in with cold hands and cheeks, glad to be in the warm kitchen and smell the pie baking.

"Your mother would have enjoyed this," my aunt said.

Yes, I thought. She would have.

Sydney Flynn

Here is the famous "Chiffon Birthday Cake" that Sydney Flynn found in her mother's cookbook. Featured in *McCall's Magazine* over 50 years ago, it was one of the most popular, delicious recipes ever tested in McCall's kitchens.

Chiffon Birthday Cake

2 cups cake flour
1½ cups sugar
1 tablespoon baking powder
1 teaspoon salt
¾ cup water
1 teaspoon vanilla extract

¼ teaspoon almond extract
½ cup salad oil
5 large egg yolks
7 large egg whites
½ teaspoon cream of tartar

1. Preheat oven to 325°F. In a large bowl, stir flour with sugar, baking powder and salt until combined. Add water, extracts, oil and egg yolks; stir just until smooth.

2. In the large bowl of an electric mixer, beat egg whites with cream of tartar until stiff. Gradually add batter to beaten whites, mixing just until combined. Pour into ungreased 10-inch tube pan; bake 65 minutes.

3. When cake is done, let it cool in pan, upside down, on a cake rack. When perfectly cooled, loosen cake from side of tube pan with a spatula. If cake doesn't drop out of the pan easily, give it a good whack on the bottom. It won't hurt the cake a bit. Miraculous? Yes, indeed!

4. To serve, sprinkle top with confectioner's sugar, or frost with sweetened whipped cream.

Serves 16 to 20 people.

Women Know

Women know
The way to rear up children (to be just),
They know a simple, merry, tender knack
Of tying sashes, fitting baby-shoes,
And stringing pretty words that make no sense,
And kissing full sense into empty words.

Elizabeth Barrett Browning

A Good Mother
Is a Child's Birthright

*Following are excerpts from a speech
delivered by Jeffrey R. Holland, then president
of Brigham Young University, at the American
Mother of the Year Convention, in Salt Lake City
on April 28, 1982. His remarks are perhaps
even more relevant and timely today.*

I suppose it's a healthy sign when someone can look at the calendar and know that despite the rhetoric and turbulence of the
last two decades, this country is still going to celebrate Mother's
Day in a week or so. That such a day of special tribute should be
scribbled on anybody's "endangered species" notepad is perhaps
the most glaring indication that the so-called "me generation" was
for a time on the verge of its worst possible expression. For when
women deny their destinies as mothers they deny destiny itself.

It is really quite stunning that except for organizations like yours,
it is painfully apparent that the value and worth of mothers have
been largely ignored. We don't have Emmys, Tonys or Oscars for
mothers. Athletes take their bows at Super Bowls and Halls of Fame.
Scientists, writers and economists have Nobel Prizes and Pulitzers.

But who cares about and honors mothers? Your organization is
certainly one. And the Congress that convened on February 4,

1914 to declare a national Mother's Day was another. But history and headlines are shamefully silent about the contributions and worth of mothers.

As Oscar Wilde said, "Anybody can make history." You only need a new tactical weapon to shake the world, or a laboratory full of rats on which to experiment, or a television camera at your disposal, or, as the NFL draft yesterday proved, just be a quarterback at BYU and sign a contract with the Chicago Bears. For these things and so many more, everyone sits up and takes notice.

But seldom have we noticed mothers. You have enjoyed virtue but been denied status. You've been happy, but as Marian Evans Cross, whose pen name was George Eliot, said in *The Mill on the Floss,* "The happiest women, like the happiest nations, have no history."

How do you get the world to notice the mother who gave her daughter the courage to run for student-body president?

Would *60 Minutes* tell the story of a widow who made baby clothes for each new arrival in the neighborhood?

Could we build a best-seller around the mother who silently but meticulously raised an honest accountant, a high school teacher, a medical doctor or a concert pianist?

Yet the sons or daughters of mothers make our society honest or dishonest, educated or uneducated, healthy or unhealthy, lovely or unlovely.

I have become quite concerned, as have others, that colleges and universities, supposedly some of the most civilizing forces in society, have failed to talk enough about such values—where we get them, how we preserve them and why society even needs them. Most often these stabilizing values come from families. And if the family is at the center of society, then what is at the center of the family? As a husband and father, I speak with authority: Clearly the heart of a family is its mother.

It is amazing to me that we assume that engineers need some education before they build bridges and that doctors must be schooled before they practice surgery. And yet those who hold together the most essential and important unit in our society—our families—are expected to succeed in that responsibility with almost no training.

As president of the largest private university in the country, I wonder if in the pomp and ceremony that goes into the awarding of degrees—and we just held our one-hundred-and-seventh commencement last Friday at BYU—we somehow consciously transmit the idea that a piece of paper, a degree—however hard it was worked for and however precious it is—could ever be more valuable than the mothers, fathers and children who live life and have responsibility for our future. We want men *and* women to get as much education as they can but not as an end in itself. We hope both men and women will use their education to bring peace and knowledge and stability to the world.

Obviously mothers, and for that matter, fathers, can only teach what they know. I don't think a woman's education—in any field—will be "wasted" if she leaves the workplace to raise a family, if she so chooses. Or if she never enters the workplace at all, again as her choice.

> Who can doubt that Abigail Smith's interest in history influenced her son, John Quincy Adams, the sixth president of the United States?
>
> Or that Katherine Elizabeth Textor's gift for storytelling was a guiding force in the life of her son, Johann Goethe?
>
> Or that Mary Ball's insistence on honesty influenced the famous story attributed to her son George Washington about never telling a lie?

Consider the memorable words of this author: "There came into the world a child of mingled Breton and Lorraine blood, who was colorless, sightless, voiceless and so poor a weakling that all despaired of him except his mother. . . . That child, whose name Life appeared to be erasing from its book, and whose short day of existence seemed destined to pass into the night with never a morrow . . . that child am I." Those are the words of Victor Hugo.

Daniel Webster's mother disregarded those who thought her son, although born with fragile health, would be a weakling all his life. Since the nearest school was several miles away and only in session two or three months a year, she taught Daniel to read before what is today considered kindergarten age. Despite his rural upbringing and lack of formal education, Daniel Webster was admitted to Dartmouth College and later became a great statesman and orator, carried on the shoulders of his mother's love.

A woman who had set out for college to study history and political science, and was voted one of the most likely to succeed, now talks about her life as a mother of nine children. "I don't think that any woman should feel because she eventually plans to marry and have a home that all of her premarital training needs to be in that specific direction. When you teach a woman, you educate an entire family. All the education you receive becomes an integral part of you—your attitudes and your approach to life."

Long before we see your sons and daughters at the university, they have already been educated and trained in values by you. We may send them sailing on a career in teaching or politics or computer science, but you have given them a foundation which we can, at best, only fortify.

A good mother is a child's birthright? Well I should say so. But what else? How many other births and how many other rights? Is it possible that a good mother is the nation's birthright? I close with this story.

> She was sometimes called Sally—a widow with three children. Perhaps life had been a little harsh and she would have welcomed a change for the better; an easier way, if it came. She thought she saw it come when a man, a widower from her past, returned with a proposal of marriage. In his nice suit of clothes and talk of a prosperous farm, the prospects of a better life grew, for she understood him to mention servants and to be a man of substance. She accepted and crossed the river with him to view her new possessions: a farm grown up to wild blackberry vines and

sumach; a floorless, windowless hut; the only servants two thinly-clad, barefoot children, the father of whom had borrowed the suit and boots he went a-courting in.

Her first thought was the obvious one: go back home! But she looked at the children, especially the younger, a boy, whose melancholy gaze met hers.

For a moment she looked, then rolling up her sleeves she quietly spoke immortal words which ought to be engraved on every mother's heart. "I'll stay for the sake of this boy."

"Oh, Sally Bush! What a treasure trembled in the balance that day," wrote one whose mother was a neighbor of the boy.

And Sally Bush didn't know when she looked at the melancholy face of ten years that her stepson Abe would someday say, as this country's most beloved and respected of Presidents, "All that I am or ever hope to be, I owe to my angel mother."

Jeffrey R. Holland

Mother's Love

*What feeling is so nice as a child's hand in
yours? So small, so soft and warm, like a kitten
huddling in the shelter of your clasp.*

—Marjorie Holmes

Ninety-three hours of labor; over nine thousand diaper changes, and two thousand children's books read—all completed in the line of mother's duty. My tasks have included: 13,000 meals cooked (not including snacks), 4,800 baths drawn, thousands of Band-Aids dispensed, and innumerable loads of laundry washed, dried and folded. Life's duty, for a mother, is like riding a carousel horse: ups, downs, and a redundant rotation of chores. In contrast, mother's love rises above and beyond the call of duty and becomes part of a child's heritage. This heritage has motivated families for generations.

Mother's love cannot be found in a family heirloom or plot of land. Nor is it the mundane repetitious daily duties mothers must perform. Mother's love does not come from the heart of just one woman. Mother's love flows from one generation to the next. A hand-me-down, an endowment, a knowledge, an identity, a solid foundation that supports the growth of character.

Mother's love is a platform on which greatness stands. Mother's love increases a child's perception of his or her identity. It is a mixture of tradition, lore, values and parenting skills. A mother's love reaches out and defies time. It flows, as sap, down the branches of a family tree. I have been inspired, nurtured and taught, in an indirect way, by ancestors I never met. Though long since past, their persons live on in the family.

I vividly recall the first instant my life was enriched by my heritage. When I was three years old, Granny would bundle me up in a soft quilt and take me upon her lap. She sat rocking and cuddling me in her arms. I stroked her arm and toyed with the folds of translucent fragile "granny skin." As she rocked, the chair rhythmically creaked. "Bye-o-baby, bye-o-baby, baby-by-'n-by," Granny sang. My ear was pressed close to her chest and I heard air rasping in her lungs, felt the vibrations and the beating of her heart. I basked in a loving, warm atmosphere created for me.

Now that she is gone, I hold a child on my lap and sing "Bye-o-baby." I try to re-create the same environment of love and surround my children with it. I practice focusing my total attention and love upon my children. Granny also had a knowing way of peering over her reading glasses. Beaming over the frames, her dark eyes would sparkle and flash rays of love in my direction. Granny gave me something more valuable than gold. She gave me mother's love.

Mother's love can be found and stored in unusual places.

One summer day when I was eight years old, I jumped down from the cherry tree that was in our backyard and ran into the house. Bored and desperate for something to do, I went upstairs. Mom had left the cubbyhole door ajar. I opened the small white door and feeling half-scared, peered into the shadows. A box of forgotten seashells collected by Great-Aunt Carrie sat blocking my path. I put a shell to my ear, closed my eyes and let the sound fill my mind. After a minute or so, I placed the shell back inside and shoved the box out of my way. When I did this another box was exposed. I opened it. The box was filled with *McGuffey's Readers*.

I carried a book out of the attic, threw myself on my bed, and began to read. I became so engrossed that I did not notice time passing. Before summer vacation had ended, I had read every book that was in the box. By asking questions of my parents, I developed an awareness of my ancestors' contributions to the local community. Great-Aunt Carrie had taught in a one-room school, just as my great-grandfather and great-grandmother had done. I also developed a strong love for *McGuffey's Readers*.

Searching through boxes of books a few months ago, I found the old *McGuffey's*. I pulled them out and called the children around me. I told them how I found the books and about their ancestors' deeds. I bought replicas of the *McGuffey's Readers* and started my children reading them. As my child sits reading nestled in my arm, I explain the historical content of the stories. I enrich the stories with tidbits of family lore. I am passing on mother's love to the next generation.

Love is also passed on in our family through handmade quilts. When I began a quilt for my son, Matthew stood, nose to the kitchen table, and watched as I spread out the fabric before him. I cut, ironed and stitched the fabric. As I pieced the quilt top together, the children watched and quizzed me. I told them of their great-great-grandmother and how she quilted for an entire community. I recounted the nights spent under Great-Great-Great-Aunt Hazel's delicate quilts. I reminded the children of the quilts their Granny made for them.

I sewed through the days and told tales spun long ago. After months of work, the quilt was finished. I draped the quilt, with a flourish, around my son's shoulders. His face glowed with excitement and he hugged the blanket tightly around himself. "It's so warm, Mommy, I can feel the love in it!" This remark melted my heart. I have succeeded in passing on my own heritage of mother's love.

Venita Parsons

Answered Prayers

There is a religion in all deep love, but
the love of a mother is the veil of a softer light
between the heart and the heavenly Father.

—Samuel Taylor Coleridge

As the youngest of five children growing up on Prince Edward Island, Canada, I felt that life was beautiful. My brother and sisters were good to me, and my mother and father loved me. I knew all that instinctively. Mother was raised, in England, to be a lady. All of her children had been born in England, and the move to Canada, just before World War I, must have been difficult for her. When the war ended, we moved to New York City.

Mother had two favorite sayings. "This, too, shall pass," she used to say, when disappointment and illness overtook one of us. "Be careful what you ask for—you might get it," was the other saying.

When I was about 11 years old, one of my playmates was seriously injured in an automobile accident. I prayed she wouldn't die. I pleaded in my prayers that she would be spared to play with me again. Finally, Jeanie was brought home and I was allowed to visit her. As I walked through her bedroom door, I stopped in my tracks. Part of Jeanie's face was missing, as was one eye. She was paralyzed down her left side, and both legs were useless. I was thankful that Jeanie's mother had followed me into the room because now she was saying, very gently, "Come, dear. That's long enough. Jeanie needs to rest."

I was tormented. Why had I begged so strongly that she live, without knowing the circumstances? I felt terribly guilty, and my mother tried to convince me that I had only done what I thought was right.

Jeanie died at home, before the month was out. It seemed that everyone, especially her mom, felt relieved that Jeanie's suffering was over. It was then that the meaning of Mother's warning, "Be careful what you ask for," became clear to me.

Over the years, there were many events that called for my prayers, and I was cautious in the wording of my petitions.

Years later, for example, when I was married and in my 30s, Mother's words again found their way into my heart. We were living in a beautiful residential area in the northeast corner of the Bronx. The people were friendly and helpful, and everyone knew everyone else's business.

There was a man among us who had lived there, with his mother, for a number of years. The young boys made fun of him, and mothers would take their little daughters by the hand if they saw him in the street. He was perhaps in his early 30s. His bright, inquiring stare made women uncomfortable, but he never did anyone any harm. Instead, he tried to be helpful. He enlisted in the Navy at the start of World War II. In only a few months, he was home again, with an "other than honorable" discharge. He was not Navy material, they said. So he helped, when he was permitted, with neighbors' Victory Gardens. He kept the baseball field in good repair for the teenagers. He led a quiet, inconspicuous life. After the local veterans returned from the war, they wanted to start an American Legion post in the area. Charlie worked as hard as anyone to enlist members and find a place for meetings. The post was finally formed and my husband, Joe, was elected the first commander. Not long after, Charlie's membership was questioned. His "other than honorable" discharge made him ineligible. Joe and a couple of others spent weeks trying to have Charlie's records changed to a "disability discharge." They were, and Charlie became a grateful and proud member of the American Legion.

One dark night, Charlie was hit by a car while walking on an unlit street. When he regained consciousness in the hospital, he was virtually out of his mind. The local hospital transferred him to Bellevue Hospital in Manhattan. When he returned home, Charlie was never the same. His life was besieged with blackouts, falls and tantrums.

He took to visiting the neighbors in their homes. Women, alone in their houses, locked their doors. One evening, he knocked on our door. My husband answered and invited him in.

Charlie just wanted to talk, and needed someone to listen. He told us his vision was badly impaired, he was seeing double. We knew that Charlie had always been an avid reader, and his extensive and beautiful vocabulary attested to that. Now he could no longer read. My husband and I were saddened by this and after he left, we talked about the unfairness of it all.

I lay in bed that night, thinking about Charlie. I wanted to pray for him . . . but what to pray for? I recall the strong emotions I had felt regarding Jeanie. How would Mother have handled this, I wondered. I started to put Charlie's trials and tribulations in sequence. He had lost his adored mother shortly after coming home from the Navy, and his sister had come to take care of him. After the accident, Charlie had lost interest in life. He didn't want to shave or bathe, or launder his clothes. His sister found him hard to handle.

I went over all the things I knew about Charlie. He was a wonderful gardener and had a magical green thumb, but after his vision problem, his doctors told him not to bend or lower his head. No more gardening.

Lying there in the dark, I came to realize that I felt a presence in the room. Somebody, or something, was listening to my story about Charlie. And I wanted to pray for him, but what should I pray for? At last it came to me. I couldn't go wrong if I prayed for mercy. And so I prayed that God would be merciful to this afflicted man. Whatever his future, please be merciful! I dropped off to sleep. When the alarm woke us in the morning, Joe and I went into our daily routine. Joe left early and I took the dog for his morning walk, locked up the house, and went to work myself.

I didn't even think of the events of the previous evening until the telephone on my desk rang. It was Charlie.

All my anxiety rushed back into my mind as I heard Charlie say, "I don't know what you guys did to me last night, but when I woke up this morning, my vision was clear! I even read your number out of the phone book!" His voice cracked as he added, "I just wanted you to know."

I was left holding the silent receiver, with tears coursing down my cheeks. I was glad I had been careful of what I had prayed for. Mother would have approved.

Anne N. Sauvé

The Healing Mother

*We are healed of a suffering only by
experiencing it to the full.*

—Marcel Proust

I grew up in West Mifflin, a small town just outside the steel mill city of Homestead in western Pennsylvania. As one of six children, I vied for my mother's attention, trying in many ways to return the love she showered upon us. She was and is a true teacher, not only in instructing us how to do things, but in molding our minds and personalities so that we would become as caring as she.

She passed on to her six children, in varying degrees, her compassion and understanding, an unrestricted willingness to help those in need, the ability to tackle head-on any problem that arose and a deep faith in God.

My Mother also had a deep love of nature, reflected in her desire to add color through a myriad of flowers that she planted on the hillside behind our house each spring. She encouraged each of us to help her with the spring planting, and I became her most ardent assistant. Throughout April and May, we would work diligently together, planting flowers and removing the rocks that seemed to be everywhere in the soil of western Pennsylvania. In late May or early June, the hillside would burst into vivid purple, pink and white, and remain that way throughout the summer.

127

With Mom's guidance, I began to read about flowers and soon learned how to identify a wide variety of them, as well as a number of weeds. The one weed that I failed to recognize, however, (although I *always* know it now) was poison ivy.

When I was 10 years old, I discovered that I was highly allergic to poison ivy. Evidently, I had walked through a patch of the noxious weed and become infected. Because of my allergic reaction, I was taken to the doctor for cortisone shots that would ease my pain, but the itching seemed to get worse and worse. It was then that I truly realized how compassionate my mother was.

When I cried, she would dry my tears. When the itching became unbearable, she would bathe me in an oatmeal solution, which seemed to ease the pain. To keep me from scratching and spreading the infection, she clipped my fingernails so short that they hurt when I touched anything. When I was feeling somewhat better, she would carry me down the stairs because my legs were too swollen and rash-encrusted for me to navigate them by myself. When she told me I was a "good brave girl," I was so proud of myself that I forgot my pain for a while. And through it all, she provided the solace and comfort that I needed more than anything.

Weeks passed and I finally recovered—although I have scars to this day from the experience. Like everything in life, this experience also had a good side, for I learned from my mother that gentle caring can be powerful medicine for any illness.

My mother's compassion, understanding and willingness to help others continue to be expressed in many ways today, particularly with my two teenage sons. Whenever one of the boys has some small problem or wants to share some small triumph, the immediate reaction is to call Grandma and discuss it with her. She provides them with a common-sense solution to the problem, a glowing reaction to the triumph and, of course, a continuing inspiration.

Margaret A. McDonald

'Til Death Us Do Part

Everything is magic in relations between
man and woman.

—Paul Valéry

Mom has a framed photo of my father on the wall in her bedroom. It's a photo she can no longer actually see, but I have no doubt my father's face is fixed in her memory like everything else dear to her. When I look at that photo now, I feel the pain and defensiveness of a man who aspired to be something more than he became. I see a terrible sadness and hopelessness in his pale blue eyes, and I no longer wonder, as I did for many years, whether or not he loved me.

I suppose that he did. As well as he could love any of the 12 of us who came along with alarming frequency and would have sapped the resources of a man far better equipped to offer a father's love. The fact is, he was not a loving father to his children, for whatever reasons. And he was not, in any way, a demonstrative person. My father was aloof, troubled, melancholy and emotionally distant.

I doubt that my mother ever thought much about the quality or nature of my father's love for her. We've never talked about it, but I believe that kind of thinking would have been alien to her. Like her mother, who emigrated from Russia to America as a young bride, she was dutiful and obedient to her husband. He was the head of the household and her partner for life—no matter how mismatched or miserable they might be. Those were the days when terms like "irreconcilable differences" or "incompatibility" were foreign notions and "'til death us do part" was a serious vow.

Besides, she was a Catholic. He was her husband, her "Bill," the only man who ever kissed her back in the days when a kiss was laden with significance. You remember, don't you? Fully clothed men and women kissed on the big screen, exchanged soulful glances and sighed softly instead of showing us their tongues as they explore the cavities of each other's mouths like starved gluttons, and then show us all their other hungry parts.

Well, I know my mother does remember those stars like Bogie and Ingrid, Katherine and Spencer and the immortal portrayals of Olivier and Oberon as Cathy and Heathcliff, and partly due to her blindness, she hasn't seen much of the other stuff.

If she could, she wouldn't like it because she's already told me "that's not love." She wasn't referring to the current crop of soft-porn movies when she made that remark recently, but to a Judith Krantz novel she listened to on audiotape. The Talking Books for the Blind service is a major source of entertainment and diversion for her, and observing what she likes to "read" had given me a lot of insight about what she thinks and feels.

And what she thinks and feels about love is remarkably akin to what I think. She doesn't like "explicit sex" for example, as expressed by Jackie Collins and Judith Krantz, not only because those books offend her (she is, after all, 85). She also doesn't like them because there's no magic and that's what love is supposed to be. Magic as in all the songs of her young adulthood, like "What is this Thing Called Love?" and "You Made Me Love You—I Didn't Wanna Do It" and so many others. And magic as in the romances she listens to by Danielle Steele or Janet Dailey, where sex is always accompanied by love.

Sometimes she'll tell me about the "juicy parts" in one of her stories—like when the perfectly formed male protagonist is feeling his "manhood." Shocking stuff, Mom. But she's a lot more comfortable with this quaint expression than the four-letter sexual terms younger women are accustomed to hearing. More important than inoffensive language, however, she wants the magic of postponement that is the soul of any true romance.

What's the magic if they don't have to suffer overwhelming desire and longing without gratification? Where's the romance if they hop on each other like bunnies just because he "feels his manhood?" And how can it be love if all they are to each other is eager, hot anatomical parts? How can it be love, Mom and I both want to know, if he isn't enchanted by her smile, her quick mind and the way she moves? How can it be love if we aren't convinced that she has never felt this way before, feels faint with happiness when she hears his voice, and would go anywhere in the world to be with him?

That's the real stuff, like Heathcliff and Cathy. I've never known any woman who didn't cry at the final scenes in "Wuthering Heights" when Laurence Olivier carries Merle Oberon from her bed to the window so she can see the moors one last time. And I've never known any man (when he's telling the truth) who didn't almost cry when Ilse tells Rick in "Casablanca" why she couldn't meet him that day in Paris years ago.

I've also never known any woman—myself included—who hasn't done some pretty insane things in the name of love. No amount of education, culture, money, intelligence or other attribute seems to influence how we'll behave when smitten. We've all experienced it at one time or another, or if we haven't, we've longed for it to happen to us. We dream about it, gaze enviously at women who seem to have it, and many of us find ways to fill up our lives without it. But, for most of us, true happiness is that elusive thing called love. The kind of love that makes your heart beat a little faster when you're young, or fills your heart with contentment when you're older. The only kind of love my mother knows about—the ultimate dream of one man, for better or worse.

I know this is damn hard to come by, but Mom is right to hold onto those dreams. It's the same dream we all share, even now when we earn multiple degrees, venture out into the world and compete with men in so many areas. It's the dream that makes smart women do really dumb things like stuff 140 pounds of mature flesh into itsy bitsy slip dresses made for 100 pounds of waif. The same kind of dumb things smart women have been doing since the dawn of civilization. Maybe we have more insight today than my mother about why we do these things, but we still do them. We've advanced to the point where we don't wear corsets to pinch our waists, but take the modern route of liposuction to flatten our tummies.

What matters is, Mom is right about the difference between the merely physical and the real thing. In our dreams, we don't have to have perfect bodies to have a perfect love. In our dreams, he's strong and caring and steady. He's Gary Cooper and Clark Gable and Cary Grant all rolled into one big guy who also has the sensitivity and boyishness of Tom Hanks or Harrison Ford.

In our dreams, he sends us flowers for no reason and, when we've been married a long time, presents us with a new diamond ring—for all the wonderful years we've shared. And, even though we're independent and competent modern women, he fills the gas tank, holds doors open for us, and fixes everything in the house or knows how to get it fixed better than we do.

In reality, maybe he forgets anniversaries, doesn't look like a movie star of any era, and can't fix a damn thing. But we still love him, and that's absolutely unshakable. And we know he loves us back, even when he doesn't behave like the man of our dreams. We just know it, in some magical, mysterious way.

The way my mother knows my father loved her.

I'll buy that, Mom.

Joan Aho Ryan

"Foodie Mom"

Cooking is like love. It should be entered into with abandon, or not at all.

—Harriet Van Horne

When I was growing up, it seemed to me that my mother talked endlessly about food. Whenever she and my father attended a party or event, she would come home and regale me with menu minutiae. When they dined in a special restaurant she would, upon her return, wax poetic about sauces, soups and souffles.

After her death in 1988, my father gave me a diary my mother had kept during a trip they made to England in 1976. They cruised there on the Queen Elizabeth II and then stayed at a hotel in London for a week. The diary was filled with descriptions of the people, the parks and the wonderful sights and sounds of the city she'd always dreamed of visiting. But most characteristically, her journal overflowed with detailed notes and jottings describing the food they'd eaten—while aboard ship, in their hotel and in London's restaurants and tea rooms.

Since she was a great cook herself, my mother was able to make educated guesses about dishes—how they were put together and what ingredients were used. In her charming way, she'd even managed to coax a few recipes from some of the friendlier chefs and maitre d's she'd met.

By the time I got my hands on the diary, I was a grown woman with a clear appreciation for my mother's love of food and her need to talk about it. Now I find I'm just a chip off the old cook, looking to connect with others who have a similar inclination.

Far from being a detriment, my own passion for the subject has led me into fascinating conversations with some of the most interesting people I've ever met. I find special joy in sharing a mutual love of food and its preparation and traditions with people wherever I go. This serves me well in my career: I write cookbooks.

It's too bad that my understanding of and gratitude for my mother's gift didn't bloom until after her death, when I finally became involved in food professionally. It makes me sad that she never knew that I became a food writer, and that my love of good food grew to equal her own.

What wonderful conversations we could have had!

What delicious secrets we could have shared!

So now, we communicate silently, and I talk to her about our shared passion—but only in my head.

Bea's Cheese Tarts

My mother, Beatrice Badash, taught me to make these appetizer tarts. They're incredibly easy to make, but they taste like omigosh.

Every time I've served them I've been asked for the recipe—usually by everyone present. Now I just keep it on my computer and print it out as needed.

When I moved to New Orleans, I began experimenting because my palate was now craving more of the indigenous flavors of my new hometown. So I added crab boil for spice, frozen and thawed artichoke hearts and fresh lump crabmeat. It's also teriffic with fresh corn scraped from the cob, and would probably accommodate any number of additions and variations. (In Louisiana, we call that "lagniappe.")

2 packages puff pastry sheets,
   thawed
Vegetable oil spray or butter
   for greasing muffin tins
1½ sticks unsalted butter
8 cups finely chopped
   Spanish onions

4 tablespoons flour
5 eggs
2 cups heavy cream
1½ cups grated Swiss or
   Jarlsberg cheese

Optional

1 pound lump crabmeat, picked
   over for shells
2 packages frozen artichoke
   hearts, thawed and halved

Liquid crab boil
Salt and pepper to taste

1. Grease three 12-cup muffin tins and line each cup with a square of the pastry. Cover with foil or plastic wrap and refrigerate.
2. Melt the butter in a large skillet and sauté the onions until golden. Stir in the flour and simmer over low heat, about 5 minutes. Remove from the heat and allow to cool slightly.
3. In a large bowl, beat the eggs and cream together. Stir in the cheese, crabmeat and artichoke hearts. Stir in the sautéed onions and the seasoning. Refrigerate overnight.
4. An hour before serving, heat the oven to 375°F. Remove the muffin tins from the refrigerator and press the pastry evenly up the sides of each cup.
5. Spoon the filling into each of the pastry cups right up to the brim, and bake until golden brown and puffy, about 30 minutes.

Makes 36 individual tarts.

Jessie Tirsch

Recipes for Living

*A good cook is like a sorceress
who dispenses happiness.*

—Elsa Schiaperelli

Whenever the aroma of shrimp Creole wafted through our south Florida home, it meant only one thing: It was my sister Maria's turn to make dinner.

Not that I should complain—at the age of six, my repertoire consisted of a variety of canned soups and sandwiches.

Mom was lucky, or so we thought at the time. With four daughters at home, she taught us all to cook at a very young age and it eased the burden on her. Aside from the basics, there were also her specialties—canning preserves in the summer, frying homemade doughnuts at Halloween, baking pies at Thanksgiving and Christmas.

Dinnertime was family time we had to respect—much to our annoyance when we were all trying to assert our independence. Twenty-four hours' notice for absence from the dinner table was a must. Supper was a time to share our day, the good parts and bad, and usually our anecdotes were accompanied by plenty of laughter.

Of course, it wasn't always a good time—like the day my five-year-old sister announced the new curse word she had learned in school. Mom was clearing the table at the time and managed to break every soup bowl in the house.

While growing up, we thought cooking was a chore. Now, entertaining is a favorite hobby for all of us, and family dinners are cherished times.

Now that we all have families, we realize that we were the lucky ones. Mom not only taught us how to cook, but how to laugh and love at the same time. I've learned through the years that there's no better recipe for living.

Andra Schabo

"My Son, the Doctor"

There are dozens of jokes about Jewish parents pressuring their sons to become doctors and the importance they place on "my son, the doctor." Here's one of my favorites:

A highly agitated Mrs. Bernstein ran along the beach, frantically signaling to the lifeguard in the distance. As she approached, she gestured toward the ocean and loudly screamed: "Help! Help! My son the doctor is drowning."

Anonymous

Going Out in Style

Be happy. It's one way of being wise.

—Colette

If there's one thing I hate, it's mother-in-law jokes. The truth is, I never understand them. You see, I loved my mother-in-law. In fact, I wanted to be just like her—a successful career woman with beautiful clothes and a natural elegance that few could equal.

Judi and I bonded the moment her son brought me home to meet her. There was never any jealousy between us, not even when the rabbi put her name on our marriage certificate as the bride. She thought that was one of life's little jokes. I thought it was one of life's little pokes, but I laughed because she did.

Judi taught me all the things my other mothers, both birth- and step-, left out.

For example, she taught me that Saturday should always be a day off. Away from work. Away from chores. Away from your husband.

Frequently, she and I would spend Saturdays together. First we'd have lunch at The Palm Court, in the Plaza Hotel in New York. Judi loved the English trifle they served, although she claimed it was impossible to enjoy the luscious British treat unless the harpist was playing at the same time.

After devouring thousands of empty calories at lunch, she'd take me over to Lincoln Center to see all the great ballet companies of the world perform. She considered this her own form of weekly exercise. But no matter how fattening Saturdays were, Judi never gained an ounce.

Jewelry was another passion of hers. The sparkles at Tiffany's dazzled her at least once a week. I must admit, I felt proud walking in the front door of Tiffany's with her because she was on a first-name basis with all of the salespeople.

Tourists would be in line waiting to buy Elsa Peretti while Judi would be asking about the salesperson's family. While chatting with them, she would examine the newest piece and ask the waiting tourists if it wasn't the most beautiful thing they had ever seen. Frequently she made a sale.

Judi loved to shop, especially at Bonwit's and Bergdorf's. She claimed they had the best designer clothes for a woman of her size, which was always a perfect size eight. In teaching me the intricacies of shopping the Two B's, she emphasized that designer clothes wouldn't fall properly if they were any larger than a six. If I dared to point out she was an eight, she'd quickly say that designers seemed to be cutting smaller these days.

Judi taught me other valuable lessons, too.

She taught me that a career woman did not have to take her husband's last name. She claimed her second husband, George, understood why she never changed her name in business after they got married. I was never sure if he minded or not. It was hard to tell because George never said more than two words during any visit. Usually, the two-word limit was used up with "hello" and "good-bye."

Anyway, I figured if her husband didn't mind that she never took his name, her son wouldn't mind if I didn't take his. He didn't. She had trained him right.

She also taught me that women are not required to cook unless they want to. And then, it should only be for pleasure. On weekends.

Every week night, Judi brought in take-out. Some nights it was barbecued chicken, other nights it was fried. Some nights it was Kung Pao chicken, other nights it was chicken parmigiana. But every night, it was chicken. She obviously took the adage of "a chicken in every pot" very seriously.

As we ate our various forms of take-out chicken, Judi would reminisce about some of the wonderful meals she had cooked—when she had time, of course. She actually was telling the truth. Her cooking was delicious—and dietetic.

What made it so dietetic? Her secret ingredients were extra garlic and Janie's Crazy Mixed-Up Salt. But unless garlic and salt are combustible, it would be more accurate to say Ex-Lax was her secret. After every one of her home-cooked dinners, the lines would form at the bathrooms. Although the food tasted delicious, it was important to skip seconds and get to the bathroom first; otherwise . . . well, you can imagine.

Judi also taught me the secret of beautiful nails. No, it was not a weekly manicure. It was a weekly housekeeper.

First she took me with her for manicures. Then she convinced my husband it would ruin my manicures if I did any more cleaning up. She gave him two choices. Either he did all the cleaning, which previously we had been splitting, or someone else could do it all. Fortunately, Rob always listened to his mother, and he helped me find a housekeeper.

But the most important thing Judi taught me was how to go out in style.

She died after a perfect day spent playing cards with her best friends at the beach. Later, they all went to dinner and laughed about how their kids were all making the same mistakes. Still later, she went home and was fixing martinis for herself and her husband when an aneurysm hit her brain. She died instantly. But she had left very specific instructions on what to do in case of her death.

We cremated Judi on a hot summer day. But we were so bereft, it took weeks before we could follow her wishes. She wanted her ashes scattered in all her favorite places: Bergdorf's, Bonwit's, Tiffany's. And the Plaza Hotel.

Each building got a small sprinkle. Just enough to always make me feel like she's waiting to shop with me. It was the last lesson she taught me: Always pick your final resting place based on where you really loved to be. After all, you are going to be there for eternity.

Erica Ress

Mabel

*The greatest good you can do for another
is not just to share your riches but
to reveal to him his own.*

—Benjamin Disraeli

The "special" child was her first child. Mother presented her as "special" to the world. I wonder how young I really was when Mother first presented her as "special" to me. We learned the Ten Commandments and John 3:16 in Sunday School, but somehow Mother saw to it that each of her children knew how to live with a "special" child from the moment we drew our first breath.

"Special" children are always served first. They are never teased and are always forgiven quickly, no matter what the circumstances or offense. They are always first in line, are loved without question, are treated with a respect far above that accorded anyone else in your little world, and every family has one.

I was five years old. Uncle Carl and Aunt Laura were visiting one Sunday afternoon with their equally large brood. In the midst of playing, it suddenly occurred to me that I didn't know which of Uncle Carl and Aunt Laura's children was "special." I stopped playing and looked over each one of those children carefully. Not one of them seemed "special" to me. Just ordinary, everyday, run-of-the-mill young ones it seemed.

I went running to Mother, apologized for interrupting her and

told her it was so very important that I speak to her. Uncle Carl
and Aunt Laura didn't have all their children yet. They didn't have
a "special" one.

She held me so close as she told me: Not all families are blessed
with a "special" child. Only those families that God can entrust
one to.

As a child I thought God had made Mabel "special." Now I
know that only Mother could have loved all of us so much that
she could elevate even mental retardation to the "accepted" rather
than the "excepted" plane.

Mabel. She was 13 years old when I was born. One of my first
memories is of leading her along a path on a summer day when
the wildflowers grew taller than my head and were kept busy with
butterflies and bees. It did not seem odd that a little child was the
protector, the caregiver to a nearly grown woman. She was as
much a part of my life as the air I breathed. It took so little to
make her happy, so very little to make her sad or angry.

Crowds, strangers, any place but home confused her and she
cried easily. It seemed that everyone in the world (except teachers and preachers) knew that Mother couldn't be at PTA meetings
or in Sunday School because she could neither leave her "special"
child alone nor take her along.

We would rush home to share our Sunday School lesson and
picture cards with Mother and Mabel, chattering like wild geese as
we all talked at the same time. Each one of us trying to be the
most important by being the loudest, we followed them from
kitchen to dining room as they carried bowls and platters and
glasses of cold milk. Then we all fell upon the feast that was
Sunday dinner.

We all have to suffer and inflict upon others the ambivalences
of the teenage years, and I was no exception. I loved Mabel and
hated her within the same hour. I was alternately proud and
ashamed of her. I was happy that she lived and angry that she had
outlived her allotted five years.

As I matured, I simply accepted her as she was. My childish
attempts to teach her to print her name having failed, I watched
silently as my children gave the same and oft-repeated lessons that

would also end in failure. Somehow the failure to reduce her status from "special" to "normal" became personal, and another generation accepted her as she was.

At 2:00 A.M. on September 16, 1978, I received a telephone call saying that Mabel was gone. Struggling with sleep, my first words were, "Where would she have gone to? Mabel never ran away in her life."

She hadn't run away; Mabel was dead. At that moment, I knew the meaning of "for now we see through a glass, darkly; but then we shall see face to face."

Mabel's life expectancy, according to the medical profession, was five years. With my mother's love and care, she lived for 56 years. She survived my mother by nine months and, I am convinced, our dear Mabel died of a broken heart.

Mary B. Ledford

The Graduate

*Character consists of what you do
on the third and fourth tries.*

—James A. Michener

I remember coming home that day, walking up the sidewalk from school. It was the spring of my second-grade year, and I had just learned that my teacher for the next year was going to be Mrs. Olsen. My brother, Steve, was in the seventh grade and of course knew everything there was to know about grade school and all the teachers.

"You better hope you don't get Olsen," he warned. "She makes you tell the time every five minutes and if you're wrong, she'll give you a swat right in front of the class! You have to do flash cards every day and if you're wrong, she makes you hold out your hand so she can smack it with a ruler!"

"Now, Steven," my mother scolded, "don't say that. Laurel, don't listen to him. Mrs. Olsen's a very nice person. None of the teachers do things like that."

My mother had been the PTA president, so she knew all the teachers. Still, I was feeling a little uneasy at the prospect of having my knuckles rapped for forgetting my times tables. So I walked along thinking about Mrs. Olsen and third grade.

Our dog, Laddie, stood at the edge of the yard wiggling about, anxiously awaiting my arrival. There was no fence there but he was well trained and wouldn't leave the yard. My father had seen to that. I gave Laddie a good scratching behind the ears and hopped up the front steps and into the house.

"Mom," I called out, "Mom, I'm home."

I turned the corner into the kitchen, expecting to proudly hang my latest paper on the refrigerator door and start searching for a snack while my mother began preparing dinner.

The two things I loved to do most were watch my mother cook and watch my father shave.

In the morning, I'd sit on the toilet seat lid and watch my dad lather up a shaving brush in a cup of soap, cover most of his brown face, then systematically shave it all off again.

We'd end these sessions by rubbing our cheeks, one to the other, and I'd tell him how smooth his face was. In the afternoon, I'd sit and tell my mother about my day and watch her delicate hands as she chopped and sliced and stirred. What a contrast these two were—she with her creamy skin and copper-red hair, he with his coal black hair and eyes that spoke of his distant Cherokee ancestry.

But this day would not be like those other days, nor would there ever be another day like those again. As I came through the door to the kitchen, I found my mother sobbing and mopping her face with a dishtowel as she neatly wrapped all her little treasures and packed them into cardboard boxes.

"What's the matter?" I asked. "Why are you crying?"

"Oh, honey," she said, and her shoulders seemed to drop in defeat, "we have to move."

Move! We can't move! My mind was screaming. We're not supposed to move, we're supposed to live here—forever. Our family had never moved; as far as I could remember, it had never even been suggested. We lived in the same neighborhood with the same neighbors all my life, and that's the way it would always be.

"What do you mean, move? Where?" I finally said aloud.

I listened to her as she explained that we had to leave our home, the only home I had ever known and thought would never change. Over the phone, she repeated the story to friends and relatives too many painful times. It seems that as my brothers and sisters and I had gone merrily along to school and play each day, my parents were fighting an uphill battle of debts and a failing business.

My dad had worked for St. Regis Paper Mill for many years when he slowly began building up his own business. He started by working as a photographer for the Washington State Patrol and learned the great demand for good private investigators.

He began by moonlighting, taking on one job at a time as he was referred by attorneys and businesses. At some point he believed he could give up his job at the mill and do his investigating full-time, while still on call to the State Patrol to photograph accident scenes. His desire to be "his own boss" led him to make a hasty and overly optimistic decision. Later, when the business began to falter, he kept it to himself until he was so deep in debt he couldn't pull himself out.

I don't know where my father was that day. My mom said he was sleeping, having worked all night. I later learned he wasn't there that day at all. Wherever he was, he was hiding—unable to tell his children that his mistakes were about to turn their world upside down.

After several moves that entailed ever-diminishing lifestyles, and with our savings depleted, my mother made the painful choice between a pride-filled husband and government assistance. Believing that her first obligation was to provide for her family, she swallowed her pride and filed for welfare.

I remember the day the caseworker brought us a box of food: big bricks of cheese and butter, real butter, and we stuffed ourselves on grilled cheese sandwiches. We went without some things, but love and faith were an abundant commodity. My mother always seemed able to find the sunny side of things, pointing out the silver lining when all we could see was the cloud. So with food in the cupboards and dependable utilities, my mother turned her sights to bigger and better things.

Here was a woman with children to provide for and no work experience or job skills. She knew she needed a way to support us, so she did what is commonly referred to as "pulling oneself up by the bootstraps." She decided she wanted to be an occupational therapist. She enrolled in college and began putting her life back together.

She studied relentlessly and came home with stories about her classes and classmates. I remember sitting at home in the evenings, watching her as she studied at a kitchen table piled high with books and papers. Sometimes she'd study with her friends, and they'd sit at the table and laugh and talk about things I didn't even know my mother thought about. I began to see her in a whole new way—not just as half of something, but as a whole person, strong and capable. And, more important, so did she.

As part of her training, she was assigned to an internship in the rehabilitation department of Good Samaritan Hospital, and that's where she set her sights.

"You wouldn't believe what they're doing for people there," she told me. "It's incredible. It would be a dream come true to work for them and help people the way they do. Patients come in after a head injury or stroke, and by the time they leave, many are feeding themselves and dressing themselves and laughing at themselves. It's just great."

I was there on commencement day and watched as she graduated with honors from the occupational therapy program at Green River Community College. I was probably too young to fully understand the lessons I had learned.

The lessons about being a woman. The lessons about pride. The lessons about commitment.

But I know I felt that day that we were going to be fine. That all we had gone through made her better able to take care of me, and made me better able to take care of myself.

My mother will retire this year after 22 years of service at Good Samaritan Hospital, helping people learn how to live with their injuries—and how to laugh at themselves. I am so proud of her.

Laurel Turner

My Dancing Days

Training is everything. The peach was once a bitter almond; cauliflower is nothing but cabbage with a college education.

—Mark Twain

My mother tried her entire life to transform me into the elegant Southern lady she personified. She failed, simply because we had very different personalities and basically, I have always been a rebel at heart. And that does not merely refer to the fact that I was born and bred in the South—Butler, Mississippi, to be exact. I have always felt it would be much more fun to perform on the stage as a dancer or an actress than to spend my life as a Southern belle.

I wanted to go on the stage and be a star since I was four years old and Mama sent me to dancing lessons with Miss Whitfield, in the gym of the girls' college. Actually, we didn't really learn to dance. But we learned to turn tumble sets, to set our feet in the five ballet positions, and to move our arms gracefully and slowly together, then apart, as though we were pulling taffy. In those days, we made taffy at home and had taffy-pulling parties. So little four-year-olds well understood these movements.

Mama made me little rompers to wear to class. We all wore little rompers. They were one piece, had elastic around the short legs, were gathered from top to bottom, and had no waistline.

149

Most of us still had baby fat and had no waistlines, either.

As I think back to those days, I can see a room full of happy children who looked like little oranges, lemons and grapes in their colorful homemade dancing clothes—laughing, learning and improvising the graceful movements that would one day mark them as elegant Southern women—the goal of every Southern mother.

We improvised in our bare feet to "Liebestraum" played on the piano. We learned to recognize and love classical music, and learned graceful movements without realizing we were being taught.

Some of us caught stage fever, and I expect I had the very worst case.

Along with dancing lessons, Mama also enrolled me in Miss Ragsdale's elocution class. This was a private lesson where I learned to memorize and recite poetry. I remember the first poem I recited in my first elocution recital on stage. It was called "The Moo Cow Moo." The first lines (which I shall never forget) were:

> My Daddy held me up to the Moo Cow Moo,
> So close I could almost touch.

But the outstanding memory of those early efforts by Mama to turn me into a lady was my first dance recital.

We had our first real costumes—handmade, of course, by the local seamstress. The occasion was a garden party for Mama's club, which consisted of young mothers who called themselves "The Mothers' Self-Culture Club." I still have some of the volumes those dedicated young women studied in the late 1920s, in order to educate themselves and their children in the appreciation of the arts.

All the children in Miss Whitfield's class, who were costumed as birds and flowers, were to take turns doing their improvisations.

I was a yellow chrysanthemum.

I could hardly wait to perform. When the pianist began my number, I eagerly emerged from behind the bushes, where all the little flowers and birds were waiting to go on.

I enjoyed every minute of my improvisation. So much so that when the pianist finished the selection, I continued to dance. She quickly started to play again, and I danced until she finished for the second time.

When it then became obvious to Miss Whitfield that I had no intention of leaving the stage, she was forced to send the little bluebird out to take me by the hand and lead me off.

I'm not sure how my mother viewed that performance. Probably with embarrassment. And that was just the first of many embarrassments she endured as a result of having a rambunctious and outspoken daughter.

Mother taught me how to let go like a lady when the dreams you held so tightly for your children don't work out quite as you'd planned.

But my mother was persistent and, eventually, she had a few successes through the years. All in all, I would have to say that as a Southern mother, she did the best she could with what she had to work with.

Betsy Bee

Letter to Kris

Alma Ralph of Elizabethtown, Illinois, wanted to teach her 17-year-old son, Kris, about self-esteem. Knowing how short his attention span could be, she decided to put it in writing.

Hi Honey,

I want to say something about self-esteem because many problems we encounter in life can be traced back to our not liking and believing in ourselves.

Every day we're either building up or tearing down our self-esteem. When we do things that make us feel good about ourselves, we increase self-esteem. We build good feelings of self-worth and increase self-confidence. When we do things that cause us to lose respect for or feel bad about ourselves, we tear down our self-esteem. Wish I had known this back when I was having temper tantrums. Each time I lost my temper, there were terrible things said and done. I hated myself afterward and all the "I'm sorries" couldn't seem to undo the impact of my outburst—on others or myself.

When a friend would call wanting me to go somewhere, or when someone invited me to a Tupperware party and I said "yes" when I really wanted to say "no," I lost respect for myself. I would get angry at them for asking and furious at myself for not having the courage to stand up for me. Not knowing how to say no,

152

usually my answer was yes, and this became a habitual pattern for me. Needless to say, my self-esteem went down with each incident.

Sometimes, I think we get the word "selfish" mixed up with "self-centeredness," Kris. Self-centered is being so caught up with oneself that we don't care about or consider the needs of others. Selfish is recognizing that one's needs must be met first before we can help others. How can I help you if I don't help myself first? How can I respect you if I don't first learn to respect me? How can I be considerate of you if I'm not considerate of myself?

Off and on over the years, I put myself in positions where I was constantly sacrificing for others, believing it was selfish to put my interests and feelings before theirs. This is the way most of us are raised and programmed as children. Well, Sweet Child, this denial of my own needs took its toll on my family and me. Ultimately, I ended up being a sacrificial lamb with no life of my own, losing sight of my true values and who I really was, doing what everybody else wanted me to without consideration of my own needs as a person.

That was not selfishness, Sweetie, but pure martyrdom. This was not selfishness, but self-centeredness. Not liking myself, I sought to please others by conforming to their wishes.

When our self-esteem is low, Bud, we try to please others, seeking their approval and attention for validation of ourselves.

It doesn't work.

When you do what's right for you and what makes you feel good about yourself, you'll find these qualities within.

And you'll find yourself free from the need to control or dominate others, and free from the need for approval from others because you're being true to yourself.

High self-esteem allows you the freedom to be who you are and allows others to do the same.

I found out something very interesting when I began standing up for myself: many times this meant saying "no." If I didn't have the money to do this or go there with friends, I was honest and told them so. If I needed to stay home and do some chores, I told my friend, "I would like to go with you, but I need to do this or that, so I will decline. Thank you anyway. I appreciate the offer."

If I had other plans or just wanted time alone, I was upfront with people and told them the truth, not making excuses or lying my way out of the situation.

You know what, Bud? Most of the time the people involved were understanding, considerate and respectful of my wishes. The people who stopped calling or coming by? Well, I realized they weren't really my friends after all.

Often I see you following in my footsteps, sacrificing yourself to be what others want you to be, and this hurts me—it leads to no good, Sweetie.

Be selfish and take time out for you.

Be selfish and take care of your needs.

Be selfish and follow your heart.

Do not be self-centered or inconsiderate of others, but selfish; for this leads to good high self-esteem, having a healthy respect for yourself and a healthy respect for others.

I love you, Honey

Mom

A Higher Calling

*A baby is God's opinion that
the world should go on.*

—Carl Sandburg

My son is 15 years old. I have been his teacher throughout his young life, from the terrible twos to the terrible teens. We have always been friends and I thought I knew him better than anyone. But he really flip-flopped matters when, at 13, he announced that he had been called to be a minister. I knew God was doing something spectacular in both of our lives, but never suspected it would be so phenomenal.

He stood before a congregation and announced his calling. I had not been forewarned! I was proud that he spoke with such conviction, but wondered secretly if it was premature or immature on his part. Did he think the ministry was glamorous? Did he really get a calling from God? Did he have any idea of the sacrifices and dedication that would be required of him?

That night, I prayed God would reveal to me whether He had called my son; I needed reassurance. I went to sleep and dreamed of a snow-white dove in mid-flight, with wings flapping gracefully in slow motion. That was it! It was my confirmation. It proved to me how independently the spirit of God moves in our children's lives. God does not seek our permission, nor give us any hint of what may occur when we turn our children over to Him.

I can think of no better advice to parents than to give their children over to God. I did, and I am still praising Him. There's never been a moment of regret, and I know my son has a true calling.

Shirley A. Franklin

Listening to Our Children

*Viola Bealmear of Sturgis, Kentucky, wrote
me a touching letter that contains a few lessons for
these troubled times. Here is what she wrote:*

I am a mother of five children—two boys and three girls. I am a grandmother of 10 grandchildren and have seven great-grandchildren. I am very proud of them all.

I always tried to take my children to church and teach them to live like the Lord wanted them to. I told them to never do things that would get them into trouble, love everybody as God so loves us, and make good homes for their families.

My oldest son is 49 years old, one son is 46, a daughter is 44 and my other daughters are 41 and 30. They are all drug-free and never smoked. I am so thankful.

I would like to say to every mother and father that when you have a little one come into your life, ask yourself a question: "What kind of life can I live to raise my baby to grow and be healthy and happy, to love others and to obey his parents?"

Show a lot of love to your children and listen to them when they are telling you something. Don't push them off. They may be needing you at that moment very much.

Maybe if we as parents listened to our children more, there might not be as many children on drugs, missing, abused and troubled. We must listen to them.

Jessi

*Children are the anchors that
hold a mother to life.*

—Sophocles

On December 4, 1989, my daughter, Jessi, was born. She is six-and-a-half years old now. The years since her birth have been filled with more worry, happiness, pride and love than I would have imagined experiencing in a lifetime before she was born. Before her birth, I did not know to what depths I was capable of loving another human being. Or what it felt like to be loved with such an innocent, unconditional love.

While I was pregnant, lying awake like a downed blimp in my bed at night, too uncomfortable to sleep, I would try to imagine what being a parent was going to be like. Always I thought of the things I could teach my child, and how I would care for it. Never did I stop to think what this child would teach me. I assumed I would be doing all the teaching.

Instead, Jessi has taught me many things.

She has reminded me that all of us are born pure and innocent. And that it is up to us as mothers and fathers to nurture that precious clean slate God gives to us in our newborn baby.

I have seen Jessi's determination and have learned from her new lessons about perseverance. How many times do we fall before we learn to walk? That kind of determination somehow fades as we get older. Jessi, with her first halting, wobbly steps, reminded me we should never give up. Eventually, we do learn to walk without falling down. The important thing is to get up and keep trying.

Jessi has brought me a gift. Just as if she handed it to me in a big box with a bow on it. The day she was born I received a second chance. A chance to see things from a child's perspective—to marvel over the butterflies, and go outside without shoes, and feel the pleasure of touching the earth. To catch myself when I say a "naughty" word, and to love surely with innocence in my heart.

But above all, my daughter has taught me about priorities. At night, when I go into her room to check on her, she is asleep with her papa bear under her arm. The complete peace surrounding her is so beautiful. I stand there for a moment and wipe her bangs from her forehead, and say a prayer that God will always protect her.

At these times, I become so aware of how insignificant the problems in my life really are. The bills, the messy house, the things I can't afford. They are so unimportant compared to my daughter. Nothing, no matter what its cost or value, could replace her. To me, that is a mother's love.

Angela Heuer-Schenk

The Amber Glass Buttons

Why is it that we entertain the belief that
for every purpose odd numbers are the
most effectual?

—Pliny the Elder

Mother was a modiste, a stylist, a buyer for the three department stores in her small home town. When her father died, during her teens, she exchanged carefree Academy days for back-breaking hours plying the treadle of an ancient New Home sewing machine. As a result of her talent and the trips to the fashion centers of New York City twice a year, the ladies of the little town were able to outfit themselves in the fashionable gowns and hats of the time.

After Mother's three younger siblings were self-supporting, she married my father, to whom she was engaged for 10 years. His meager salary as County Judge, and more lucrative income from selling fire insurance nights and weekends, made it possible for her to sew only for her family and close friends.

One day a package arrived from Aunt Minnie, Mother's younger sister. It was for me and contained four amber glass buttons shaped like little bowls from a child's tea set. Mother and I were going shopping that afternoon for material for my new winter coat.

"How nice!" Mother said. "There are four buttons; we'll use three and have a spare one."

An opinionated six-year-old, I shouted, "No! I want four buttons on my coat."

"Three are more stylish," Mother said. "An uneven number of buttons is better. Always remember that."

And I always have!

Unfortunately, we couldn't go shopping because Mother got a bad headache. Later that afternoon, she died suddenly from a cerebral hemorrhage.

After the funeral, Aunt Minnie took the amber buttons home. A few weeks later she sent my coat. She made it of dark brown corduroy. The buttons were just right for it. But she made it double-breasted: she used four buttons. It was not stylish! I cried and cried and no one knew why.

To this day I never see buttons on anything without counting them and thinking of Mother. I know I always will.

Elizabeth Thomson

Domesticating Dorothy

*The pursuit of perfection, then is the pursuit of
sweetness and light. . . . He who works for
sweetness and light united, works to make reason
and the will of God prevail.*

—Matthew Arnold

Domesticating Dorothy was not an easy task. I was that
Dorothy, and I'd rather play baseball or go to a football game
than practice domestic arts. I resisted any suggestions that I learn
such skills.

My sister Mary, who is five years older, loved to cook and sew,
skills she learned at an early age. Mother didn't push me to learn
cooking mainly because she didn't want me messing up her
bright, shiny kitchen.

Memories of seventh and eighth grade home ec are not happy
ones. I recall burning muffins, pouring split pea soup down the
drain when the teacher wasn't looking, and waiting for a sewing
machine with my color so I wouldn't have to thread the machine.

For some reason when I was 13, my mother decided I should
learn to sew. Since my sister was planning to make a dress, it
seemed a good time for me to make one, too.

What power I felt when Mother allowed me to select any pattern and material I liked! While I wasn't enthusiastic about the
ordeal to come, I did like the idea of choosing what I wanted.

Mary and I went shopping for patterns and materials. She chose a sheath dress with a matching jacket that had a collar and three-quarter length set-in sleeves. I decided I'd use the pattern, too.

Next, Mary chose a lovely tissue gingham plaid. I always wanted whatever Mary had, so I chose a plaid, too (not the same one, however. Mary didn't want me to have a dress just like hers. My plaid was more complicated.)

It wasn't long before I learned Sewing Rule #1. Always buy plain materials. You have to match plaids. Later I learned Sewing Rule #2. The lesson for collars and set-in sleeves should be reserved for advanced sewing class (advanced into the 25th century, in my opinion).

My mother supervised the cutting of the garments. In fact, she did most of it, laying out and pinning the pattern for me. We had to match the plaids, and she didn't want me to ruin it before I had hardly started.

Pumping the sewing machine at break-neck speeds when I came to a straight seam was all the fun I had. I could zip that up in record time. The only trouble was my seams were usually crooked.

My perfectionist mother would say, "That won't do. I'm afraid it will have to be ripped out."

After ripping the seam and sewing it up again for the fourth time, I'd object. Mother would say, "You want it to look right, don't you? You'll want it to look nice when you wear it." How could I argue with such logic?

When the seam was finally straight enough to satisfy mother, she would inspect it closely. "Your seam is nice and straight, but the plaid doesn't match here and here and here."

"I don't care!" I was defiant.

Quietly my mother would say, "I'm sure you wouldn't want to wear a dress looking like that. Put it away for now. You can work on it again tomorrow."

Sometime I became "Jack the Ripper." I grabbed the scissors determined to fatally slash that dress and jacket. Mother would rescue the garments just in time.

"You are tired. Put your sewing away. It's coming along. I'm sure you don't want anything to happen to it after all of your work." My mother's logic again.

Finally, after what seemed like a historical era, I finished the dress and jacket. The seams were straight, the plaids matched, the sleeves fit smoothly and the collar stood up as it should. I was truly proud of that outfit, and so was my mother. I wore it with pride. I had made it.

No, this sewing experience didn't domesticate Dorothy. It was many more years before that happened. It was a long time before I engaged in such a project again.

However, during those sewing lessons Mother taught me not only how to sew a straight seam and to match plaids, but also to have patience, to never give up no matter how many adversities, to finish the task I started and to have pride in my work. Perhaps most of all she unwittingly taught me how to get along with a perfectionist, and that was good preparation for the 50 years I spent with another perfectionist, my husband.

Dorothy M. Reese

Proverbs and Prayer

Nothing ever becomes real till it is experienced—
Even a proverb is no Proverb to you till your Life
has illustrated it.

—John Keats

Mother quoted Proverbs as though she wrote the book. "Pride goeth before a fall" kept us from becoming puffed up no matter the size of an accomplishment. "Listen to your father and mother. It will gain you many honors" (and listen we did). "The value of wisdom is far above rubies." "A good name is more to be treasured than silver and gold." We could identify with wisdom and a good name but doubted that rubies and silver and gold would ever be a problem with which we would have to deal.

We found a whiskey bottle along the road and a bit of the amber liquid was still in the bottom of the bottle. Never one to miss an opportunity to teach, she poured the few drops in a bowl, struck a match and as we watched with amazement as the liquid burned, she quoted the Bible's promises of doom for users of "strong drink." She sealed the fear firmly by challenging us "to imagine what that burning liquid would do to your stomach."

Mother took the Bible literally and went into the closet to pray privately. But if you knew the owner of the article of clothing she

165

held in her hand, you knew for whom she was praying. To find an article of one's own clothing in her hand would lead to much soul searching and unspoken promises to be "good" as mother would have us be.

During the years of the second World War we often found her caressing a sailor's uniform as she prayed and the war became real again to children who forget so easily. On the day her first son returned from that war, we recognized him from way down the road. We relieved him of his duffel bag, dancing around him all the way to the house. All of us talked at the same time in an attempt to tell him all that had happened in the years he was gone. What we were really saying was, "Welcome home, big brother, welcome home."

He and Mother greeted each other in trembling silence and she then introduced him to the little sister who was born while he was gone.

Mother would later utilize the fine wool material of one of those Navy uniforms by taking it apart at the seams and steaming it carefully. She cut and sewed her last little daughter a fine winter coat with a red-lined hood.

Mother was a member of the Episcopalian Church. Daddy was Baptist. Someone recently asked me how then I became a Methodist. The answer to that question is really very simple. The Methodist church was the only one within walking distance.

The same Methodist Church celebrated "Family Day" every year. But after several years of the Baird family walking off with all the prizes for "The Youngest Child," "The Oldest Child" and "The Family with the Most Children," it was agreed by the congregation that "Family Day" would no longer be celebrated until some of the Baird children grew up and left the community.

Mother never abandoned her use of Proverbs as a guide to living. She chose for her tombstone, "Her children shall rise up and call her blessed."

Mary B. Ledford

A Mother's Prayer

The greatest of all blessings
Comes from a mother's prayer
As she places her children
So lovingly in God's care.

Though many are the dangers
That must be faced in life,
A mother's faithful prayer
Protects them all from strife.

For it matters not at all
Whether far away or near,
The sound of her prayer
Echoes forever in God's ear.

And when life is finally ended,
God will certainly declare
The gates of heaven be opened
Because of a mother's prayer.

Eva Marie Ippolito

New Tricks

Peering through the lace curtains
of the dining room
overlooking the two-rut driveway
beside the house,
we witness the third day
of mother's bicycle-riding lessons
self-taught.

Movie camera ready,
we document the process
giggling in disbelief.
The mounting,
the takeoff,
the half-pedal,
the loss of balance,
the landing on the soft grass
between the tracks.
Maximum trip:
ten feet.

"Forty-eight is too late."
She never learned,
but only quit trying
when she knew we were laughing.
Yet we were proud
that she tried.

Jane Mayes

What's a Mother to Do?
Circa 1941

fix breakfast,
rich smell of coffee
beckoning up the open stair
a molecular alarm clock
intruding upon dreams
of flying over the electric lines
get daddy off to the linotype
give us this day our daily pie
a cake will last two
dinner at noon
clean up and see if you can
get everything done in the afternoon
but it never works that way

do the washing
sometimes all day Monday
lucky you have an electric wringer
it makes life much easier
ironing Tuesday
Wednesday special projects
spackle the worn toilet room linoleum
paper the hall wall

sew up a dress for daughter
(when gramma spent the trimester
you got off darning and mending)
paint a cupboard
make drapes/wash & stretch curtains
spade the garden
shovel the walk
(save daddy's heart so
he could outlive you by
a lonely eight years)
thursday do-gooding
visit a shut-in
clean the church basement
clerk the rummage sale
sew altar cloths for the missions
Friday is scrub the floor
dust the stairs down
never up
fresh doilies
dust the cellophane on the lampshades
and candles in their holders
(someday special we may light them)
we break for our-lady-of-perpetual-help
devotions
Saturday smell of fresh bread and
doughnuts smoking bubbly in the grease
kids get some holes rolled in sugar
bake extra for the weekend
you never know who may come by
wash our hair with pine-tar soap
confess your sins
your lustful longings for laziness
weekly bedtime baths
Sunday Mass
serve the Lord
and serve our dinner
after dishes

your reward
an hour of classical music on the radio
with apples and popcorn and your feet up
before you made us supper

you finally sat down
to read the paper and fell asleep
with it spread out in your lap
good-night
God bless you &
don't forget your night prayers

Jane Mayes

Contributors

Betsy Bee recently retired from her position in the Executive Office of the Governor of Florida, where her employment spanned 10 years and three governors. Now launching a second career as a writer, she has written a number of stories about her family, which began as gifts to her children and grandchildren. Some of these stories have been published in the *Tallahassee Democrat*.

George E. Burns is an intrepid private pilot who has supported his habit as a public relations man for Pan American World Airways, Trans World Airlines and Citibank, though not all at the same time. He lives in New York City.

Jeffrey R. Holland was ordained a member of the Council of Twelve Apostles of The Church of Jesus Christ of Latter-day Saints in June of 1994. Previously, from 1980-1989, he served as the ninth president of Brigham Young University in Provo, Utah. He is a former Church commissioner of education, dean of the College of Religious Education at BYU, and instructor at several institutes of religion. A native of St. George, Utah, Elder Holland and his wife, Patricia, are the parents of Matthew, Mary Alice and David, and the grandparents of two.

Allan Kalmus spent eight years at NBC-TV as the nation's first television publicist. Subsequently, he became publicity director at Lever Brothers Company. For the past three decades, he has run his own public relations/sports marketing agency in New York City, and has represented Bob Hope for 33 years.

Joel Kimmel has been a licensed psychologist in Coral Springs, Florida for the past 17 years. In addition to his private practice, Dr. Kimmel serves as a psychological consultant to corporations on issues including workplace violence, health promotion, employee conflict resolution, and purchases and manages EAP services for these corporations. In his rare moments of leisure time, he is collaborating on a novel.

Jane Mayes is a retired teacher and high school librarian. She lives in Port Austin on the tip of Michigan's "thumb," where she and her husband raise Standardbred harness horses. A mother of three grown children, and a first-time grandmother, she published her first chapbook, *Impressions,* in 1993. Mayes' poems have appeared in two anthologies, as well as magazines and newsletters. Her column, "Lit., etc." appears weekly in the *Port Austin Times.*

Carol Moser is divorced with one married son and resides in Manhattan. Since the closing of her advertising agency, Anders Moser O'Brien, she has been freelancing as an art director. Her interests include cooking, working out and travel. She is presently writing a book on breast cancer.

Venita Parsons is a freelance writer, the mother of five children, and the wife of an Air Force officer. A resident of Ohio who was raised in Kentucky, she has written for *Woman's Work, Family, Green Prints: The Weeder's Digest,* and *The Brooking Line American Chapter.*

Leonard Pitts Jr. joined the *Miami Herald* as its pop music critic in April 1991. Since 1994, he has written a syndicated column on family and social issues. Prior to 1991, he was a writer for Casey Kasem's radio countdown program, *Casey's Top 40,* in Los Angeles. Pitts has been writing professionally for 20 years and his work has been featured in such publications as *Musician, Spin, Soul, Parenting* and *Billboard.* He is also a writer and producer of radio documentaries on subjects as diverse as Madonna and Martin Luther King Jr. Pitts' work has been honored by the

Society of Professional Journalists, the American Association of Sunday and Feature Editors, the National Association of Black Journalists and the Florida Society of Newspaper Editors, among others. He was a finalist for the 1992 Pulitzer Prize and is a 1977 graduate of the University of Southern California with a degree in English. Pitts is married and the father of five children.

Erica Ress is a creative director in advertising in New York City. While flying around the world creating a campaign for Procter & Gamble's Pantene Pro-V, she became bored and quit to attend Tulane Law School full time. Her solid credentials in marketing soon presented her with opportunities to handle clients in New York while attending law school in New Orleans. Fortunately, this hectic life is almost over and she hopes to add "Esquire" to her signature in 1996. She says it will take another wonderful mother-in-law to convince her to try marriage again.

Claire Safran writes on social issues, celebrities and human drama for major national magazines. Her most recent book, *Secret Exodus,* is a dramatic account of the secret rescue of the black Jews of Ethiopia. Her writing has been recognized with a number of professional awards, including the American Society of Journalists Authors Award for the most outstanding magazine article; the Williams Harvey Award (twice); the Odyssey Institute Award (twice); Matrix Awards from Women in Communications; and a recent Deadline Club citation for investigative reporting.

Liz Smith is a nationally syndicated columnist based in New York City. Her distinguished career in journalism includes posts as entertainment editor for *Cosmopolitan Magazine,* associate producer NBC-TV, staff writer for *Sports Illustrated Magazine* and commentator with WNBC-TV and Fox-TV. She is a recipient of The Emmy Award, and author of *The Mother Book,* published by Doubleday in 1978.

Debbie Smoot is a beloved writer. *Reader's Digest, Guideposts* and many other major magazines and newspapers in the United

States have published her work. Her works are available throughout the world in many languages. She resides in Salt Lake City with her husband, David, and their three children—Owen, Emily and Amy.

Jessie Tirsch is the coauthor of *Emeril's New New Orleans Cooking* (William Morrow, 1993). She is currently at work on a cookbook depicting the culinary traditions along the Gulf of Mexico, tentatively titled *Gulf Coast Gumbo*, which will be out in Spring 1997 from Macmillan Publishing. In addition, Tirsch is penning a cookbook for McGuire's Irish Pub in Pensacola, Florida. A native of New York—one of the world's great food cities—Tirsch now resides where the food is no slacker—New Orleans.

Yustin Wallrapp heads a management consulting firm based in Massachusetts, specializing in the marketing and communications fields. He was formerly the president of two international public relations agencies. He is a contributor to a wide range of business publications and is a frequent speaker on business topics.

Bettie B. Youngs, Ph.D., Ed.D., is one of the nation's most respected voices on the role of self-esteem and its effects on health and wellness, vitality, achievement and productivity in both the homeplace and workplace. She is the author of 14 books published in 27 languages, including *How to Develop Self-Esteem in Your Child: 6 Vital Ingredients, Safeguarding Your Teenager from the Dragons of Life, Stress and Your Child: Helping Kids Cope with the Strains and Pressures of Life* and *Values from the Heartland*. She can be reached at Bettie B. Youngs & Associates, 3060 Racetrack View Drive, Del Mar, CA 92014.